THE

MAKING OF AMERICA

SERIES

CRAWFORDSVILLE

ATHENS OF INDIANA

One of the beauties in the 1916 Centennial was Eleanor Ristine, pictured here showing her patriotism. Eleanor was a descendant of one of Crawfordsville's first citizens, Henry Ristine.

THE

MAKING OF AMERICA

SERIES

CRAWFORDSVILLE

ATHENS OF INDIANA

KAREN BAZZANI ZACH

ARCADIA PUBLISHING

ISBN 978-0-7385-2417-7

Published by Arcadia Publishing
Charleston, South Carolina

Printed in the United States of America

Library of Congress Catalog Card Number: 2002116806

For all general information contact Arcadia Publishing at:
Telephone 843-853-2070
Fax 843-853-0044
E-Mail sales@arcadiapublishing.com
For customer service and orders:
Toll-Free 1-888-313-2665

Visit us on the Internet at www.arcadiapublishing.com

FRONT COVER: *The Pinewood Derby Boys, shown here, are possibly at one of the contests during the Fall Festival Parades held each August in the 1920s. The location is the corner of Washington and Wabash Streets in Crawfordsville. Note the long poles to "push off" the drivers. This picture was most likely taken by Nicholson & Sons Photographers, who took many early photos of parades and other public scenes.*

Contents

ACKNOWLEDGMENTS

Crawfordsville: Athens of Indiana was chosen as the title of this book for the simple reason that members of our fair city have always strived to further culture. As far back as 1836 in the *Crawfordsville Record*, our first county newspaper, cultural activities were reflected. These included the inauguration of Wabash College's first president, the functions of literary societies, and in a July edition that year, the first mention of this description of the city. William Compton, a leading citizen, toasted Crawfordsville at the Fourth of July celebration: "To Crawfordsville: may she be as prosperous as her citizens are enterprising and liberal." The influence of our many writers, our all-male liberal arts college, our cultural organizations, our many politicians, and our varied businesses and industries have all shown the truth of Compton's title.

The writing of a book is not an easy task but the gracious people of our community have given much cooperation in creating this work. Special thanks to Dellie Craig of the Crawfordsville District Public Library for her relentless scanning of the majority of the early pictures of the city and its makers. Thanks to the library staff members, especially Dian Moore and Bill Helling. Knowledge I obtained from Bridgie Brelsford and Joyce Jones via books and discussions practically wrote chapter two. The Andy Robinsons and Frank Powerses were helpful in writing sections as well. Mike Hall, Anita Hardwick, Joan Spragg, and Chandler Lighty provided information about two of Crawfordsville's most important citizens, Henry S. Lane and Lew Wallace. Picture credits also go to Archie and Alberta Krout, Ernie Patrick, Clela Jones, Dave Shaw, and Virginia Servies. Special thanks to my local and not-so-local editors, Lena Carlson, Reed Morrow, Tracy Jones, and Martha Lewellen. Others needing thanks are Jeff Scism, Dave Long, Johanna Herring, Dale and Linda Petrie, Suzie Baldwin, Bill Degitz, Vic Powell, Joan and Bill Zach, and Jacob and Becky Hurt. In fact, thanks to anyone else who has helped me in writing this book in any way.

Final tribute goes to my wonderful husband, Jim, of 35 years, who has taken pictures as well as provided general help for not only this project but many of my brilliant and not-so-brilliant endeavors in the past. He understands and encourages my need to know and share history. It is our hope that our children and grandchildren carry on this tradition.

1. The Birth

Ambrose Whitlock was quite an adventurous soul. He platted the town of Crawfordsville and about a dozen families purchased lots there in March of 1823. Born in Virginia in May of 1767, he joined the Army at age 21 and soon became a commanding officer. He assisted in the building of Fort Washington, now the city of Cincinnati. Elizabeth Jones, his wife, had a brother William who owned the first hotel in Vincennes. Although the Whitlocks had no children, they were surrogate parents to several Jones nieces, one of whom, Janey, lived 54 years in the Whitlock homestead.

Whitlock was with General Anthony Wayne in the process of opening up Indiana to white settlers. According to Beckwith's *History of Montgomery County*, "As Major, he served as a paymaster where he carried his funds in keel-boats to the military stations on the Mississippi, Ohio and Wabash Rivers, amid the dark domains of savage life." In the War of 1812, Whitlock commanded a company of volunteer scouts outside of Vincennes. About 1817, he retired to civilian life.

The first government site for the sale of Indiana land was set up in Vincennes and later moved north to Terre Haute. In 1822, another move north for the sale of land was needed. Secretary of the Treasury William H. Crawford (head of the Public Land Office) appointed Whitlock as receiver of public monies. Whitlock suggested a town in its forming stages. This of course became the city of Crawfordsville. There was an earlier tale that Crawfordsville received its name in honor of Colonel William Crawford, a Revolutionary War soldier from Virginia. He was surrounded by Wyandotte Indians and burned at the stake. It seems much more likely that Whitlock named the new town after his longtime friend William H. Crawford of Georgia. John Q. Adams wrote that the receivers of public monies and land registers of land offices were "the most active electioneering partisans in Crawford's cause," so it is safe to say Crawfordsville received its name from this Crawford; however, the romantics lean more toward the story of Colonel Crawford and his untimely, tragic death than that of the man who lost the 1828 presidential election.

According to H.W. Beckwith's *History of Montgomery County*, the town's original territory was described as follows:

> Each street running North and South is laid parallel with the North and South line of Section 31 and 32. Each street and alley running East and West is laid out parallel with a line dividing townships 18 and 19. Each street within the lots is 65' wide except Market and Washington Streets which are 95' wide. Each alley is 10' wide and a reservation of 60' as a street is made all around the town, except from the south side of Spring Street to the Northeast corner of town. Each lot within the town is 165' by 82' 6".

The infant town was made the seat of government of Montgomery County and, for judicial purposes, over all the land lying north of Montgomery County to the southern shore of Lake Michigan. At the time Crawfordsville was born, it was the only town between Terre Haute and Fort Wayne, with the District Land Office in the center of the tiny settlement. Williamson Dunn was soon joined by Whitlock in the Land Office. It is interesting to note that Dunn's great-great-granddaughter Janet Cowan compiled a wonderful collection of all Crawfordsville Land Office sales over 150 years later.

Williamson Dunn was appointed register by President James Monroe and brought his family from Jefferson County, Indiana to the new town; however, he was not a stranger to the area. Williamson Dunn had been born in Kentucky in 1781, married in 1806, and was probably in what is now Montgomery County

Ambrose Whitlock founded Crawfordsville. Whitlock platted the town and served as the first receiver of public monies in the Federal Land Office.

Williamson Dunn, first register of lands at the Crawfordsville Federal Land Office, sold land for 17 counties. Earliest land records show that an acre sold for $1.25.

as early as 1813 when he was a captain of rangers (along with Ambrose Whitlock and Henry Ristine) and returned to be with Whitlock and his land office. Dunn remained at the land office until late 1829 when Samuel Milroy replaced him. The Crawfordsville Land Office sold lands for Benton, Boone, Carroll, Clay, Clinton, Fountain, Hendricks, Monroe, Morgan, Owen, Parke, Putnam, Tippecanoe, Vermillion, Warren, White, and of course, Montgomery, making Crawfordsville truly the "Crossroads of Indiana."

Sanford Cox, early schoolmaster, noted the quick influx of people as he entered the following into his diary on December 24, 1824:

> The land sales commenced today and the town is full of strangers. Ohio, Kentucky, Tennessee and Pennsylvania are strongly represented. There is but little squabbling as the settlers have arranged matters among themselves . . . $1.25 per acre is Congress price . . . it is a stirring, crowding time here, truly and men are busy hunting up cousins and old acquaintances. If men have ever been at the same mill, or voted at the same election precinct, it is sufficient for them to scrape an acquaintance upon. Sales continued to flourish as can be seen by the 1830 Land Office sales totaling $367,146.39.

The final sale at Crawfordsville was made March 26, 1853. Thereafter, the Indianapolis Land Office took care of unsold land.

Henry Ristine was the first inn-tavern keeper in the city. He was also a county commissioner and state legislator.

William Miller erected the first cabin inside Crawfordsville limits and other cabins began to appear along present-day Green and Market Streets. Miller and a man named Matthew Cooley had cut their first wagon trail from the Big Raccoon Creek to Crawfordsville in 1822. An old Native American trail from the Ohio River to the Wabash River to Big Raccoon Creek had been used. The first settlers existed with the barest of necessities, living in crude cabins built of rough logs. Cracks were mud-chinked. Good land, a healthy location, and plenty of clean water were their goals.

Lying just outside the original town plat were several natural springs said to possess medicinal powers. Whitlock purposely reserved these springs for public use and built his residence immediately above them in a beautiful grove. The area at this time was so wild that if a person stepped off the few trails, he could easily become lost. Whitlock gave 3 acres of land for a cemetery (Old Town on Grant Avenue). He also designated "school lots."

The Federal Land Office was housed in a log structure on the north side of present East Market Street, just west of the railroad crossing. Whitlock told those coming to the land office lacking a few dollars, "If you are honest you will pay me without giving me your note, and if you are dishonest you will not pay if you do give me your note." Jim Leas in *Montgomery County Legend and Lore* called him "The Poor Man's Friend." Leas pointed out that on a trip to Washington, Whitlock went to the Treasury Office for a settlement of his land office accounts. He noticed the clerks there had made an error amounting to $50,000 in his favor, and in calling their attention to it, he told them, "You don't know how to keep books here." They told him to get out. He did but returned with Treasurer Crawford, who agreed with Whitlock. Leas wrote, "Whitlock Avenue and a tombstone in Oak Hill Cemetery are monuments to the founder of this city. Perhaps there is another, certain to be recognized by any student delving into the community's history and that would be Crawfordsville itself."

When Crawfordsville was just one year old, it had what was probably its first business, a tavern and inn kept by Major Henry Ristine. Ristine was born September 4, 1781 at Albany, New York of Dutch descent, the eldest of eight children. He moved to Kentucky and there married Nancy Gray on Independence Day in 1805. In the War of 1812 a company of about 100 men traveled the Wabash River area, including where Crawfordsville stands today. Williamson Dunn was their captain, Ristine their lieutenant. Ristine was said to be the first Whig elected from our county.

There was also a grocery belonging to Jonathan Powers, two stores (Smith's and Elston's), a lawyer (Providence Curry), and his brother Thomas, who was one of two doctors (along with Magnus Holmes). William Nicholson owned a tannery, Mr. Scott and Mr. Mack owned cabinet shops, and George Key had a blacksmithing business. "A small mill was ran by an Old Man Hill," according to Sanford Cox's diary. Perhaps 50 families lived in the vicinity of the infant city. "With each passing year, the growth of settlers continued, the mighty forest thinned and a new breed created a new world!"

James Wilson, son of John Wilson, was said to have been the first white child born in Crawfordsville. He became a leading lawyer associated with Dan W. Vorhees and Benjamin Harrison. In fact, Wilson later beat Vorhees in a race for Congress. James's son John Lockwood Wilson was a graduate of Wabash and a U.S. senator. Later, Wilson was appointed minister to Venezuela, where he died and was buried. His remains were eventually moved to Oak Hill Cemetery—back home again in Crawfordsville, Indiana.

The home of William Miller was the site of the first circuit court with the Honorable Jacob Call presiding and all proceedings taking place within until the first courthouse was built. Cox wrote, "the building was on Main Street, was 26' long by 20' wide, made of hewed logs and was two stories high." As with many of the early buildings, native poplar planks were used. Cox continued, "the lower floor had two doors and four windows, the upper floor having three windows with 12 panes each. Eliakim Ashton built the impressive court for $295."

The first proceedings took place on August 28, 1823, when John Toliver was indicted for assault and battery. Oddly, this structure lasted but a short time due to ever-increasing county business and was replaced by a structure almost four times larger than the original. John Hughes built this courthouse for $3,420. It was brick with a square cupola in the center of the roof. This structure lasted until

1873 when a large Berea sandstone, brick, and iron building with jury rooms and offices was constructed in its place. This was built for $124,000 but the large clock in its tower propelled the cost to $150,000.

In the early 1900s, folks came to town to go to hearings, just for the entertainment of it. In Pat Cline's *Pictorial History of Crawfordsville*, there is a tale about this. Cline wrote, "Those who weren't satisfied with the judicial system sometimes settled their disputes in an alley behind the courthouse. That alley became known as 'bloodshed alley' because of the many confrontations staged there." She also states that, "When Montgomery County's third courthouse was completed, Lew Wallace predicted that within 50 years the new structure would be too small for the growing community." Of course, we all know that it is still being used today, but there have been ongoing rows about the building, recently the annexation of space. Also, many desire the courthouse tower to be replaced. In fact, Dr. James Kirtley spent many of his later years raising money (including giving all proceeds from his autobiography) in order for the clock tower to be restructured. Sandy Lofland carries on his work today.

To go along with the courthouse, a jail was essential; thus a suitable building was erected. Being the same width as the courthouse and only 2 feet less in length, the jail also had double walls added. It contained two rooms, one for felons and one for debtors. Abraham Griffin built the structure and received $243 for his work. The first inmate was Peter Smith who was accused of stealing a silver watch. Although the jail was quite adequate for its time, one stormy night our first felon burned the lock of his cell, gained access to the other room, made his escape, and left the new jail to its fate of fire. Our first sheriff S.D. Maxwell promptly recaptured Smith and chained him up in the courthouse where he stayed until his conviction. His sentence? Three years of hard labor in Jeffersonville Penitentiary.

At the time of the 1830 census, Crawfordsville showed a population of 422. There were over 100 houses in the town a mere one year later, according to the *Crawfordsville Record*. "There is a great demand for houses here. Every house is full and some have two and three families in them." Four hotels were filled to capacity at $1.50 per week. *Record* editor Isaac Ferris Wade noted the only complaint was "too many dainties." He wanted more cornbread and vegetables!

Wade had come from Butler County, Ohio, after hearing reports that Crawfordsville was a booming Land Office town. Wade's enterprise was welcomed with enthusiasm. Early pioneers craved news, particularly about their home states. James Heaton, county recorder from 1848 to 1852, lived in the 500 block of East College, and his sister Aletha married Wade. Wade owned the first monument company in the city and was likely the first to sell fire insurance as well. The Heatons had 12 children and the Wades had 7. Wade's daughter Sarah married A.P. Luse of a longtime family of newspapermen. The Indiana Historical Society now owns the Heaton-Wade letters.

Charles F. Bryant served as Wade's printer and editor. According to him, "many crowded the newspaper office on October 18, 1831, as the first newspaper rolled off the press. Isaac C. Elston, Postmaster, was one of the first to take advantage of the advertising columns, by printing an unclaimed letter list." Although Wade would not support any political party, he did advocate education and religion. Holmes and Harlan bought out Wade in a few years and closed *The Record* in 1837.

It was just after the 1830 census that the Indiana General Assembly approved an act allowing towns to incorporate. Of particular interest in the text of this law was: "It shall not be lawful to retail by less quantities than one quart, spirituous liquors, or to keep what is commonly called a tippling house without a license from the county and another from the town." Sometime in the year of 1831 Crawfordsville was incorporated for the first time, but the actual date is not known. However, in January, 1832, *The Record* shows excerpts from letters to the editor regarding the incorporation of the town:

> I see a notice in your last paper, stating that the corporation of Crawfordsville has been dissolved. This is quite strange. I never knew a

This drawing by Lydia Stewart, Turkey Run High School student, shows the first courthouse in Crawfordsville.

> petition had been in circulation. I cannot believe a majority of citizens are in favor of it. Perhaps some were afraid that a tip or two of their money would be spent in improving the streets or the like, which I suppose they think altogether unnecessary. And others maybe were afraid that the corporation righteously tax them for keeping up groceries (a barroom). Cursed be those who giveth his neighbor strong drink that putteth the bottle to him.

A reply stated:

> I would like to know in what dark corner this gentleman lives. The petition was made just as public as it could be . . . let him examine into the cause which led to the dissolution, and he will be able to conceive why any man living in town should wish to have this corporation dissolved. Groceries are already taxed. He speaketh of them being the hotbeds of crime. He seems to intimate that with a corporation we would have none of the crimes. What is our experience? Directly to the contrary!

To get another view of Crawfordsville about this time *The Record* noted that there were doctors and lawyers, but they usually had other professions because "no one got sick and everyone got along." Although cholera and other infectious diseases

This is one of the many boathouses found on early day Sugar Creek. The creek served as a living for many boating enterprises and provided recreational opportunities for other community folk.

were fairly common in those days, the pure water and sanitary conditions "kept Crawfordsville remarkably exempt from epidemics." The paper stated further, "money is seldom loaned for less than 50% which shows that business is lively."

Will Hughes kept the first livery stable and furnished horse, saddle, and bridle for 50¢ per day. There was even a wedding apparel store kept by Ira Crane. Merchants of the day traveled to Cincinnati, Buffalo, and Louisville to purchase goods. In turn, grain from the area was driven by wagon to Chicago for sale. Always a hotbed of divorce, Crawfordsville was still an infant community when there were two divorces tallied in 1829. George Southhand divorced his wife Jane, while John Monroe divorced his wife Jane. Perhaps they were Plain Janes?

Finally, the red-letter day was October 14, 1834, when Crawfordsville was again incorporated with Henry Ristine, president of the board; Isaac Naylor, secretary; and trustees Chilion Johnson, Jacob Angle, and Caleb Brown. Although a temperance league already existed and was quite active (66 members strong), the first city ordinance gave $8 liquor licenses to "sell intoxicating liquor" in the town, but with the stipulation it was to be sold in small quantities. Another exciting happening was a public auction in this year. A bull brought $3, three horseshoes 39¢, a pieced quilt $1.50, and a red petticoat $1. Auctions are still quite popular with Crawfordsvillians today.

According to Frank Mills's *Early Days in a College Town*, his father came to Crawfordsville about 1835. Frank's parents had sold a farm at Ladoga and moved to Crawfordsville where Mr. Mills leased a hotel on the corner of Main and Washington. He also purchased a grocery. A bar was attached to the grocery, but Mills, being a teetotaler, poured out all the whiskey. A census that year tallied 269 males over 18, 221 females over 18, 226 males under 18, and 261 females under 18. With 17 African Americans, the total was 994 people in town.

In 1836, a circus visited Crawfordsville with exhibitions under a 100-foot tent. There were horseback riders, clowns, and other acts. In 1837, many residents suffered great financial losses, and many "took the benefit of the Bankrupt Law," according to Mills. A popular recreation even in 1837 was "the old swimming hole," located in the middle of Sugar Creek with its 4-foot table rock, but "the deep hole" a hundred yards away was the terror of many a mother according to Frank Mills. He said in the wintertime, entertainment was sleigh rides or ice skating on Sugar Creek.

In the fall of 1841, *The Review* (the Democratic paper) published its first issue. The *Journal* (Republican) came into existence three years later and the two were competitors until they finally merged almost 100 years later in 1929. Several other newspapers were in existence for short times, including *The Examiner*, *Peoples' Press*, *The Locomotive*, and *Tomahawk*, but these two were the major ones. Lucky for Crawfordsville, The *Journal-Review* continues to inform us of local events.

Mills were important in those days, easy access being one of the reasons the site for Crawfordsville was chosen. The Sperry Mill was one of the earliest and operated well past the turn of the century. There were water-powered saw, grist, and woolen mills, as well.

August Vogel, a German immigrant, created some of the most beautiful coverlets ever woven. Here is an example of his exquisite work.

In 1844, Teddy Brown, Frank Mills, and 13 others were members of a Whig Glee Club. They sang at many political meetings in and around Crawfordsville. Throughout town about this time, Hetty Conrad "was the daily huckster of vegetables." According to Mills, J.Q. Warner, a watchmaker, was one of the town characters: "He always carried a gold-headed cane. He was slim, wore a tall black hat and usually a black tight-fitting suit. He had only one suit at a time. If it got unwearable in winter, he bought a heavy winter suit, thus wearing a heavy suit in the summer."

Getting across Sugar Creek up to 1846 was accomplished by boarding a ferry boat. That year, a large covered bridge was built. Also this year, William P. Watson built a tannery on what was known as Lafayette Pike at the edge of town. An over-shot water wheel and a branch that used to run by the Pike furnished the power. It was closed about 20 years later.

One of the most prominent of businessmen during the 1840s was August Vogel, born in Saxony, Germany on October 31, 1801. He came to America to ply his trade as a weaver, immigrating because of European industrialization (power looms, in particular). Vogel applied for citizenship in 1836 in Franklin County, Indiana but had been in Crawfordsville by 1848. Naturally, his occupation was listed as weaver in the 1850 census. At age 53, he married Nancy Byers. An exceptional weaver of fine coverlets, rugs, and blankets, he died in January 1859.

It is estimated that Crawfordsville had about 1,500 souls during the 1850s. An actual citizen count was done for the city in late June of 1865, and the tally was 2,316 inhabitants. This census was done for the explicit purpose of incorporating the town. On August 10, it was voted 188 to 27 to make Crawfordsville official. Hotels were numerous and filled to capacity in this era. The Virginia House ran by Calvin and Ann Walker and the Hotel Taylor House under the proprietorship of Reuben and Jemima Taylor were two such establishments.

On September 4, 1865, an election was held. Wilson Laymon defeated George Snyder by 91 votes to become the first mayor. Quite a versatile man, Laymon had served as a captain in the Civil War (Company F, 86th Indiana Volunteers), was a graduate of Miami University in Ohio, and practiced law for some time. He served as editor of several papers, was owner and operator of a grocery business, and after serving as mayor, operated a local restaurant. Oddly, Laymon had lived in Crawfordsville a mere 13 years before being elected its first and following mayor. Laymon's salary as mayor was just $600 a year. During his mayorship, the city police department was organized to enforce the community laws.

Other first city officials included the following: clerk, T.D. Brown; assessor, John Franklin; treasurer, William Burbridge; engineer, Daniel Roderick; marshall, John Ross; councilman, first ward, Benjamin Wasson (who beat John Speed, who tallied only one vote but oddly won the third election for mayor); councilman, second ward, William S. Fry; and third ward, William Epperson. According to Beckwith's history, "in the May 1868 election, a city attorney [John W. Ramsay] was added. In the 1880 election, the total vote was 1,009 versus the 351 fifteen-years before at the city's first official election."

An interesting series on the naming of our streets written by Emmy Peebles can be found in late 1983 and 1984 *Montgomery County Magazine* articles. Additions to Crawfordsville go back as early as 1829 when Williamson Dunn added 20 acres (northwest of the original plat) to the town. Almost yearly, Crawfordsville added more property. A big boom in 1836 resulted in a total of 11 additions. The next year, Wabash College added almost 100 acres to the town and John Pottinger extended the town by 30 acres. No other additions were added for six years, then almost yearly several lots were added up through about 1880. It was projected at that time that the improved property could "accommodate a population of 20,000," which is about the Athens of Indiana's population today.

The Sperry Mill, an early mill in the city, was in operation into the 1900s.

2. Warrior Whoops

Much of the information regarding Native Americans in the Crawfordsville area is pure legend. Some of the more credible stories are included here, but all are advised to read with caution!

Likely the most famous of the area Indians was Peter Cornstalk; however, there is some debate as to his true identity. In Bridgie Brelsford's excellent work, *Indians of Montgomery County, Indiana*, we learn of at least three major candidates for the Peter Cornstalk who roamed the area near Parkersburg. It should be noted that Cornstalk stories are numerous. He is purported to have warned a white family in Terre Haute that other Indians were planning to kidnap their red-haired child, and he taught settlers to cure snake bites near Wesley, Montgomery County. There are enough tall tales to make us wonder why he doesn't rank right up there with Johnny Appleseed or Paul Bunyan.

It is likely that Peter Cornstalk was a Miami Indian named Ahsonsong, and his contact with white settlers here took place from 1822 to about 1830. His village is thought to have been on Cornstalk Creek near the Old Harshbarger Cemetery. According to Brelsford, an 1820 surveyor's map locates Cornstalk Town at about this location in the northeast of Section 34, Township 17 north. According to old settler's stories and historian W.L. Anderson, the Cornstalks were:

> Somewhat migratory but made their chief residence five miles southwest of Ladoga near what is now the Cornstalk Baptist Church on the bank of Cornstalk Creek. The church was possibly plopped atop the Indian town. Artifacts were found in Section 22, Scott Township on the bluff over Cornstalk Creek, so this perhaps was the site of Cornstalk's village.

As with Cornstalk the man, Cornstalk the village was also controversial. Yet, we can keep in mind that being migratory, members of this community likely came here during the winter for hunting and sugaring, moving their village each year and spending other seasons elsewhere.

Although Anderson reported that the Indian villages in Scott and Clark Township were deserted in 1828, Brelsford believes that Cornstalk was here until at least 1830. According to *The Ladoga Pioneer* of September 15, 1887, a letter

The Cornstalk monument is located in Parkersburg, Indiana. Cornstalk was an area Native American.

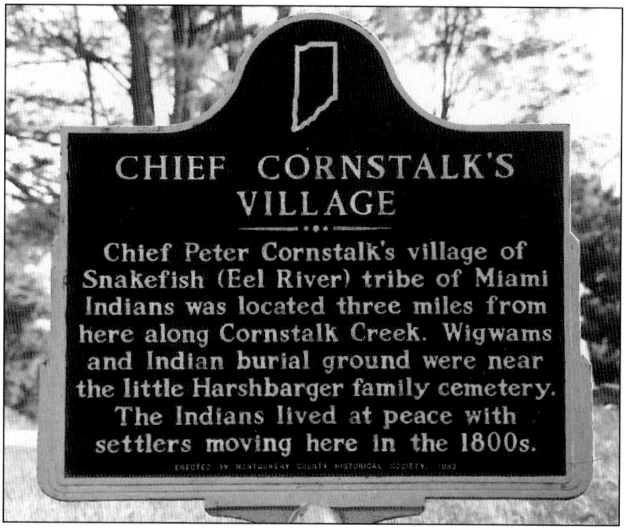

written by James H. Harrison stated, "Cornstalk, Chief of the remnant tribe of Indians then living near my residence at Old Cornstock town informed me of the time for the sale." Also, Brelsford's research of the land the 1820 Cornstalk Town lay upon showed that the land had not been "settled" (only owned by out-of-towners) until at least 1833, which suggested the Cornstalk family still hunted there after the 1830 Thorntown sale.

Much research has been done on Peter Cornstalk and his little band, yet little is known, not even where he went after leaving Montgomery County. There is a connection between Cornstalk and the Thorntown Miamis. Since Cornstalk told James Harrison, a young pioneer boy in Montgomery County, about the land sale, and a signature of Awsawonzawgow (which could be viewed as Cornstalk's Indian name, Ahsonsong) who was Chief of the Eel River (Thorntown) Miamis was on the 1828 treaty, it is probable that he was the same person.

In the county of Howard, the post office, Cornstalk, and Peter Cornstalk Creek were named for "an old Miami of the Thorntown band, who lived in the vicinity." Cornstalk was merely a nickname used by the white settlers. His proper name Ah-son'-song meant "Sunshine." And it certainly takes a lot of sunshine to make those corn stalks grow.

By all means, Cornstalk was not Montgomery County's only Native American to view our early settlers. An old Potawatomi Indian, Shick Shack, told of a battle in which he fought on what is now Shades State Park. This took place in September 1775 between the Miami and the Potawatomi/Kickapoos. There were over 600 chosen warriors battling, but when the conflict was over, only 12 remained, and Shick Shack was one of them. Even the Great Tecumseh likely passed through the area as he often made treks from Terre Haute to Lafayette. County lore says that there was an old sweathouse on William Miller's land in Walnut Township. This may have been Miller's makeshift home of two rail pens

Some area Native Americans battled at Shades State Park. Pictured are the "Falls" at the Shades, depicting the area in its more virgin timbered state.

heated by a blazing log between them. Indians would run into the structure to sweat out any illness, then dash to the nearby creek.

Another old Indian named "Strap" lived on a branch of Walnut Creek. His small group remained here only a short time after the first settlers organized Walnut Township, about 1831. Andrew Davis's biography relates, "Strap got his name because he wore a strap on his nose to cover up a bad cancerous nasal passage." Indians were in the Wingate area, Ripley Township, South Union, Clark, Wayne, Coal Creek, Scott, and Madison Townships. A tale has been passed down about an unnamed Native American squaw in South Union Township coming to the aid of William and Jennie Offield as Jennie gave birth to one of their older children, the first white child born in Montgomery County. Evidence of Indians was found in the mounds of Franklin Township where skeletal remains and artifacts were found in Sections 23 and 34. Many pieces from our area have been found, but sadly few were tagged as Montgomery County artifacts by various museums. We are lucky that Joyce Jones, one of Montgomery County's most knowledgeable Indian lore scholars, has just opened an Indian Museum in Waynetown, Indiana.

Residents and visitors to the area should keep in mind that if arrowheads are found here, they are not from the Potawatami or Miami group in our area—as they would have used guns—but instead date back to a much earlier period. The paleolithic periods began when woolly mammoths roamed the earth. This was up to about 8,000 B.C. These Native Americans took over tundra areas and coniferous forests, hunting big game. Fluted points with narrow vertical flukes are distinctive to this era. Today, these are rare.

Toward the end of this time came the Archaic period, from 8,000–1,000 B.C. New tools allowed the nomad to have a more stable village life. Projectile points in this era were more triangular, stemmed, or notched, and didn't have the earlier fluted edges. In the mid-Archaic period, Indians began to grind, smooth, and chip their tools. From 1,000 B.C. to 900 A.D. the Woodland Tradition was dominant. These Indians fired clay pots and cultivated the ground, plus they had elaborate burial grounds. Dramatic changes could be seen in the projectiles from the earlier points. Smaller, thinner, triangular ones now came into existence.

From 900 A.D. to 1600 A.D. was the Mississippian period when the groups existed in more town-like states. Farming for squash, beans, and maize helped with existence in the fortified villages. Elaborate pottery and ornamental artifacts are from this time. Small, lightweight projectiles were used as arrowheads. They were made from flint and were used to hunt game as well as the enemy; however, there were no reported incidents of violence from the settlers in regards to the natives in the area. According to Brelsford, "The small remnant of Indians in the county accepted the inevitable. Their retreat from the beloved hunting grounds was sometimes slow and sullen but there was no resort to violence."

Joyce Jones, a specialist in area Native American culture, recently opened a museum in Waynetown.

3. Immigration—Emigration

Most of the immigrants to Mongtomery County were Irish and it is well known that many left Ireland because of the potato famine. But why did they come to this area? As many as 160 came to Montgomery County in the potato famine years, between 1843 and 1847, with several arriving directly thereafter. Of the foreign born in the 1850 census, all were Irish except two from France, five from England, seven from Scotland, fourteen from the German provinces, and one from Africa. Many of those here at that time tended to stay, but the main reason for the arrival of the Irish was that they found work on the Monon railroad. Many Irishmen followed the building of the railroad. They often stayed in an area to their liking or where they found other jobs and could put down roots.

Irish immigrant Henry Tammany, a railroad contractor born in Ireland, had 13 railroad families living with him in the 1850 census. Twelve heads of these families were born in Ireland. Tammany's total assets were an unbelievable $70,000. Especially in the Catholic Cemetery, the Irish roots can be seen.

Of the 2,563 immigrants to our county before 1900, 1,463 were Irish. In the 1870 census alone, 571 Irishmen were found, with 327 of those living in Crawfordsville and 109 more in Union Township. They weren't just railroad workers, especially as late as 1870. Other occupations were farmers, stone cutters, bakers, launderers, coopers, weavers, merchants, cabinet makers, government office holders, and even college students. An interesting Irish immigrant was Maurice Campbell, born on August 22, 1841 in Donegal, Ireland, the son of Alexander Campbell. He was still young when he died on August 15, 1874, but he already had quite a reputation about Crawfordsville. According to his obituary, Campbell was known as Cheap John:

> Until he was 17 years old he spent his time in the routine duties of farm life; but his inclinations were in a different channel and he early conceived the idea of immigrating to America, where he could carry into effect his plans for trading with the people. But, how to pay for the voyage? The labor he performed on the farm was due his father. Even if he had received wages the amount would have been small and time would lengthen into years. He determined upon a much shorter

> method, being borrowing from his father. Thinking it unnecessary to speak to him about it, he went to his father's trunk on the afternoon of Sunday, August 27, 1858 and took out $50. Without saying goodbye to father or mother he started. At Donegal he took a jaunting car, (similar to a livery) for Londonderry, 48 miles further. The ride cost him two shillings (50 cents). At Londonderry he sailed across the English Channel to Liverpool. On the 4th of September, he set sail from Liverpool to the United States, landing in NY on the first of October. Twenty of the $50 was now gone. He left New York for Wheeling, Virginia where he had a brother. After spending a few days visiting, his brother provided him a small pack of table linen and notions. He came over into Ohio and commenced his pilgrimage of traveling from house to house to dispose of his merchandise. He was quite successful and by Christmas he was able to repay the money he had "borrowed" from his father and $25 interest.

In August 1860, Campbell came to Crawfordsville where he remained until his death. He commenced the spectacle trade the first year he was here in a small way, selling only the cheap quality. His trade rapidly grew and with it he increased his stock both in size and quality until he had succeeded in introducing into the county the best spectacles made—the celebrated glasses manufactured by George Staples. This branch of his business he made a specialty. "Cheap John" was known to every man, woman, and child in Montgomery County. His obituary continued: "By his failing fund of good humor, his social qualities of head and heart and his fair dealing in business he succeeded in building a trade that many prominent business men envied."

Bernard Kennedy, builder of the old Catholic church, was probably the most influential as far as the Irish community. The altar was hand polished by the parishioners. One fireplace kept the churchgoers warm. The total cost of the church was $800. Kennedy aided Father Edward O'Flaherty, the first resident priest for Crawfordsville in 1859. The church was a necessity due to the ever-growing Irish Catholics. With O'Flaherty's aid, there had been many good times for the community's Irish. It is said that St. Bernard's partially received its name because of the hard work of Bernard Kennedy. In the Crawfordsville area today, we still see Irish related names from these immigrants, such as Calhan, Clements, and Foley. Of course, not all Irish were Catholic, and not all Catholics were Irish, but the Irish population did indeed make up a large chunk of Catholicism in this era.

Next to the Irish in number of immigrants would be those from the German countries. One of the mayors of Crawfordsville, Fred Conred Bandel, died while serving in office on January 5, 1897, having been born in Strausberg, Germany April 26, 1851. His obituary stated that he was a man "of kindly heart and genial soul . . . a man of courage of his convictions, yet conservative and considerate of rights of all men." As a boy, Bandel helped his family by selling papers on holidays and vacations because his father had died young. Fred learned the stonemason trade, then came to Crawfordsville in the 1870s. Coming because of his masonry skills and thinking to pass on after the jobs were over, Fred soon fell in love with the city and stayed. On July 24, 1875, he married Lena Steinhouse and, by 1893, he was nominated by the Republicans for mayor. He won by one of the largest majorities ever given in the city. In 1894, he was renominated under the new law for a four-year term as mayor, again being elected by a large vote. From the obituary: "Commendably fair with rare wisdom, he was a tireless political worker. He was a Knight Templar, Odd Fellow, member of Knights of Pythias and Order of Ben Hur." Reverend Dr. Leech said to him, "As much as your wife and children love you, God loves you more than they." So, after bidding his family an affectionate farewell, he passed on.

The Lorenz Brewery was one of the first and largest industries of Crawfordsville. It is said that the beer cellar dug in 1864 still extends back under Market Street today. Dellie Craig of the Crawfordsville library researched the Lorenz Brewery for a descendant of the founder and discovered that Henry Lorenz was born on June 9, 1827 in Germany. He immigrated to the United States as a young man, first locating to Hamilton County, Ohio. From there, he came to Crawfordsville. In 1853, Lorenz purchased an old brewery located on the triangular-shaped property encased by Lafayette Avenue at Market Street and Grant Avenue (northeast corner), which was at the time the western boundary of the town. When the building was razed in 1924, an old copper box was found in the cornerstone of

St. Bernard's Catholic Church and St. Charles Academy building were located on the southeast corner of Pike and Washington Streets.

the brewery, which was from Lorenz's 1865 remodeling. In the box was a $1 gold piece, a $5 gold piece, an American flag, a *Weekly Review*, and a *Weekly Journal*, among other things. Almost the whole town was there for the 1865 dedication. A quartet sang, a minister blessed, and all members of the Lorenz family struck a blow with a steel hammer on the cornerstone.

The brewery's beer was brewed for 24 hours, then run into the huge hogsheads that were stored in the cellar under Market Street. From the hogsheads, the beer was drawn into 4- and 8-gallon kegs, then delivered to their retailers. Lorenz was a prominent citizen of the community, serving on the city council. His five children, Adolph, Mary, Caroline, William, and George, were left without parents as Henry's wife had died two years before his death in 1870.

Another prominent German Crawfordsvillian was Anthony Kostanzer. Born in Heckingen, Germany on September 10, 1819, Kostanzer came to Crawfordsville from Lafayette in 1849. He built his home/furniture store at the corner of Washington Street and Wabash Avenue, the original building being replaced a few years afterwards. He and wife Jeanette Appkins had 13 children. Kostanzer made many hand-carved pieces to order and there are several inlaid pieces of his work still in use. While the handmade furniture of that day was not as elaborately finished as the parlor pieces of today, it was made from the finest woods and was very substantial. Such goods could not be made today, for the timber is unobtainable.

At that time, there were no coffin factories in this part of the country and Kostanzer also made coffins, many made to measure. His work gave satisfaction and his methods brought many new customers. The Kostanzer Furniture Store can be remembered by many today and was one of the longest standing firms in Crawfordsville. The store was operated by Anthony Kostanzer and his sons John and Herman, then Paul of the third generation of the family identified with the store. It was said of Anthony that he lived a life of great honor and was diligent in business. From a humble beginning, he built up an independent fortune. The Kostanzers were prominent businessmen for many years to come, dealing not only in furniture, but in shoes, carpets, rugs, linoleum, and electricity as well.

English immigrants rank next. The Englishmen were so prominent in the county that it's hard to choose those to include. One prominent citizen was William E. Brown, born in Manchester, England on November 22, 1853. Brown contracted out to work on the farms of Alexander and Hugh Meharry. The Meharry's parents had been Irish immigrants. Brown farmed for some time in that area, but then came to Crawfordsville where he was a bridge carpenter on the Big Four Railroad, finally becoming the superintendent of the county poor farm.

A much older Englishman was William Cook, born on March 31, 1793 in Kirton, England. A descendant of Cook, Helen Ernstes of Indianapolis, wrote that William and his wife Elizabeth (Nailor) started for America with their family of four sons and two daughters, but 18 days out of England, the ship sprang a leak and they had to return to shore. Many people were leery of reboarding the ship, but the Cooks reset sail and arrived in 1852, settling in Montgomery County, Ohio for a short time. Mrs. Cook and one son died and were buried there. Part of the family headed west to Montgomery County, Indiana and settled on a farm 6 miles northeast of Crawfordsville. William was not naturalized until October 1870 and was still living in the 1880 census.

One of our early doctors, William DeCraux Tilney, was born in Norwich, England in July 1841. You may learn more about him and others in *Montgomery Medicine Men*, available from the Montgomery County Historical Society.

Another one of our old settlers was Richard Breaks, born June 5, 1791 in Yorkshire, England. He was one of the earliest to be naturalized in our county, doing so on September 19, 1831. He said there were but six cabins in Crawfordsville when he arrived. With 50¢ in his pocket, he said he built a cabin across the creek from a Native American village and worked for Andrew Beard. Purchasing a small farm, he became a prominent farmer in the area and is buried in the Breaks Cemetery, having died September 5, 1870.

Next in line in foreign births would probably be Canadians. Some of the names (Crull, Davidson, Dale, Doherty, Fuller, Fulwider, Hutton, Kehoe, Kennedy, Kirkpatrick, Lyon, McJimsey, Neff, O'Brien, Oliver, Pool, Rafferty, Roach, Rowe, Scott, Shelby, Shephard, Sweeten, Trask, and Trout) are familiar to Montgomery County folks today.

Dr. Samuel R. Peacock was born on June 15, 1867 in Oakville, Canada. Dr. Peacock grew to manhood in Ontario and graduated from the University of Buffalo in 1892. He came to Ladoga in January 1894 and his brother came to Darlington. Sam married Lois B. Walterhouse on June 6, 1900. He was said to have been plain, unassuming, hardworking, friendly, and "always a student." Sam was a Mason and staunch Democrat.

Scottish folk would round out the last of the bigger influxes of immigrants. A prominent Scot was William Robertson. Born August 7, 1821, a native of Cooper Angus, Scotland, he died in August, 71 years later. Only nine when he came to America, his family resided at Cincinnati where he thoroughly mastered the cabinet maker's trade. Arriving at manhood, he drifted westward and worked at his trade in Iowa for some time, then arrived in Crawfordsville about 1851. For several years, he was associated with Thomas White and Thomas Ross in the furniture and undertaking business. During the war, he was with Frank Cox and P.H. Burns on the corner of Wabash Avenue and Walnut Street. They were burned out in 1868; a new firm was formed on a larger scale, Captain R.E. Bryant being taken into this firm. For many years, Robertson was actively engaged as superintendent of the great coffin factory.

The best known of the Crawfordsville Scots was John Speed. There is hardly anyone in Crawfordsville who has not heard of the Speed family. John was born in Pertshire, Scotland in 1801 and married Margaret Baxter. He came to Philadelphia in a codfish schooner. He was a stone cutter and worked on the capitol's stone steps. Having heard a new state house was to be erected in Indiana, he started here and arrived in 1834, but was disappointed that he did not obtain

This building housed the county's poor for many years. Located at the end of Whitlock Avenue, English immigrant William E. Brown was superintendent there in the late 1800s.

work in Indianapolis. He wandered throughout the state and decided to make his home in our little city. His family settled down here, but he did some traveling in order to ply his trade. The whole Speed family were radical Jacksonians, as well as intense Abolitionists. Known as a harborer of runaway slaves, he hid them in the garret of his house. One time there were so many "extras" that Speed bought 25¢ worth of bread, then sent his children throughout the town buying small amounts of food until he could finally feed the slaves and send them on their way. Although the Speeds had several children, their son Sidney became as well-known as his father. Having attended Wabash College, he served in the Civil War, fighting his father's cause against slavery. Both John and Sidney Speed served as mayors of Crawfordsville.

Although there weren't many French-born people who came to the Crawfordsville area, there was Eli Kahn who had a clothing store in Crawfordsville, as well as Peter Fisher, a cigar maker. John Fishero was born in France about 1816 and seemed to be quite a fine cabinet maker who lived in the Alamo area.

No more than a few Swiss, Swedes, Russians, Chinese, and Italians entered our Athens city, but be assured, each and every immigrant left their mark upon the county. Today, many from Mexico are among our most current immigrants, with some from Asia. Yet, it is most fitting to end the story of immigration to Crawfordsville with the Greeks. Uppermost among them is of course the Harry Siamas family. Siamas came to America from Greece in 1923. Many Crawfordsvillians will remember him as the owner of The Coney Island. John Siamas, son of Harry, was a local policeman. One of his feats was to arrange security for George Wallace, who spoke at local churches while campaigning for

A portion of the Speed home is currently located on the grounds of Lane Place. John Speed's home served as part of the Underground Railroad, as noted by this historical marker. (Photo by Jim Zach.)

the United States presidency. John's sister Areta married Martin Kaitson, another Greek immigrant. Martin managed the Carrico Furniture Store for some years here. Following in his father's footsteps, Harry, son of John Siamas, is also a public servant. He is a lawyer, while serving on many local boards. Harry and his lovely wife Suzanne are some of Crawfordsville's most active volunteers.

Need your shoes fixed? The Gianakis family has been in the shoe repair business in Crawfordsville since 1921. Harry John Gianakis, born on the Island of Crete, came to America in 1908 "to see gold on the streets," as many there believed. He spent some years in New York before settling in Crawfordsville where he heard a shoe repair service was needed. Knowing nothing about it, he soon became an expert. In 1935, Harry returned to the Greek Islands to find a wife. After two dates, he returned home with Mary, his wife for many years before his death parted them. In 1954, Army surplus items were added and soon along came camping equipment, guns, and clothing. The store originally was at 205 East Main Street and, in May 1969, the New York Shoe Repair and Bargain Center moved to its present location. John, a 1957 Crawfordsville High School (CHS) graduate, began working for his father Harry at age seven. Four generations of Harry John's family have made Crawfordsville proud.

It is well known that the majority of the early Montgomery County settlers emigrated from either Fleming County, Kentucky or Butler County, Ohio. This was largely due to government land postings in those courthouses. Once a family member decided to come here, other family and community members followed.

Peter Binford from Virginia owned almost 2,000 acres, and the Vances from Ohio had about 700, as did the Stoddards from New York just above Crawfordsville. Other men who purchased several acres in this area were James Boyd, Fred Bronson, Josiah Halstead, and Jonathan Potts.

Below Crawfordsville in Southern Union Township were more land owners, owning fewer large parcels. Many names are still well-known in the area today: Armantrout, Brooks, Burch, Chesterson, Davidson, Dunn, Everson, Faust, Fitzpatrick, French, Graham, Guntle, Hamilton, Johnson, Kelsey, Lamson, Leak, McLaughlin, Oliver, Powers, Ramey, Richardson, Riddle, Surface, Thompson, Warren, Wilhite, Williams, Wilson, and Wray. These families mostly hailed from Ohio, Kentucky, Pennsylvania, Virginia, Tennessee, New York, North Carolina, and New Jersey. The majority of the early settlers of the county were from Ohio or Kentucky.

Probably 16 volumes on the many important settlers of Crawfordsville could be written, but let's use Edmond Nutt as an example. He came to Crawfordsville in 1822. His feet were his mode of transportation and he found the country densely wooded. He thought that he walked on an old Indian trail to the city where he placed his claim to land. He told his children that there was a great abundance of touch-me-nots. Quickly, he cleared 40 acres and went back to Ohio for two years. Again, he came to Montgomery County, this time on horseback, but he was shocked at the growth of the area. At that time, corn brought 12¢ a bushel

Harry and Mary Gianakis were Greek immigrants. They raised their family in Crawfordsville where Harry owned a shoe repair business, now owned by his son John.

and pork 25¢ per hundred weight. Nutt chose a Montgomery Countian for his bride. Marrying Elizabeth Mann on May 10, 1828, they became parents of seven children. His son William Nutt, born in Union Township on April 22, 1844, owned Nutt's Hotel, which was a beautiful old brick building on the corner of Green and Market Streets. In 1959, Elston Bank & Trust purchased the property, while destroying the building to make a drive-in bank. Today, the CVS Drugstore is at this location.

The Nutt's Hotel was located on the northwest corner of Market and Green Streets. It was torn down in 1959.

4. Lincoln, Lane, and Lew

Many parallels can be found in the lives of Abraham Lincoln, Henry S. Lane, and Lew Wallace, some obvious and some not so. Lincoln, Lane, and Lew were all lawyers, at least for a period of their lives. Wallace studied under his father David, one-time governor of Indiana. Lane's main profession was law, studying under a cousin, James Suddeth in Kentucky. Lincoln, as we all know, was self-taught and had a prosperous law career in Springfield, Illinois.

Lincoln, Lane, and Lew were all politicians. In every history book, we read the story of Lincoln running for and obtaining a congressional seat, losing the election against Stephen Douglas for a Senate seat and finally his election to the United States presidency.

Henry Smith Lane was born 10 days after Valentine's Day in 1811 in Montgomery County, Kentucky. He came to Crawfordsville in 1833. Two years later, he was elected to the Indiana Legislature from Montgomery County. He was elected to Congress in 1840. To show his popularity, it should be known that he beat his opponent by 1,500 votes. Lane was a Whig until the Republican Party was formed in the 1850s. His popularity with his peers soon became evident as he was chosen president of the 1856 Republican National Convention held in Philadelphia. In 1860, Lane was nominated for governor by his party. While campaigning, he took time out to attend the convention at which Lincoln was nominated.

Although Lane won the governorship and gave great promise to be a worthy and popular one, he was only governor for four days before he resigned to become a United States senator. In Congress, he was on the committee of military affairs where he voted for needed supplies and was a most passionate Union man. After his term, he retired to his home with such great men visiting him as Schuyler Colfax, Vice President of the United States; Governor Joseph A. Wright from Parke County; Chief Justice Harlan; and Dan Vorhees, criminal lawyer and United States senator, who began his law career under Lane's tutelage. Lane's home was of course what all Montgomery Countians know as the Lane Place and once home from his senatorship he never again ran for public office. His home thereafter served as a "political mecca." The March 20, 1912 *Northwestern Christian Advocate* of Chicago described the Lane Place:

> Wooded, embowered, and hospitable, Lane Place lies in quiet dignity in the very heart of the "Athens of Indiana;" not with slight propriety since the people of this historic homestead have been held in veneration and love of the city throughout all the years of a quarter of a century. This is the home of the late United States Senator Henry S. Lane. For natural beauty and historical associations it shares with the homestead of the late General Lew Wallace, author of *Ben Hur*, the interest of all visitors to the city.

Lew Wallace's political career is not as glorified, but nonetheless deserves mention in a history of Crawfordsville. One interesting point regarding Wallace was that, for a short time, he attended Wabash College Preparatory School at about age nine. It is interesting to note that Wallace received an honorary degree from Wabash in later years. After the Mexican War, he returned to his hometown of Covington and set up practice there. Today, there is a group working on the restoration of the building that housed his law practice. In 1852, he moved to Crawfordsville. He was elected a state senator, but served only one four-year term, finding political life not at all to his liking. Wallace served two terms as prosecuting attorney of the First Congressional District, which provided service for a six-county area.

All three men were exceptional orators. Lincoln delivered the famed Gettysburg Address, along with numerous other speeches. Lane was said to have had a great and fiery voice and showed much enthusiasm in regards to the topics at hand. Bowen's history states the following:

> As an orator, Lane had few peers in his day; he was convincing and often truly eloquent. As an extemporaneous speaker, he never cared whether his addresses were printed or not. He always interested and instructed his audiences at the same time and swayed them as one man. He showed prowess in mustering troops, where he used earnest logic to convince, not only during the Mexican War, but the Civil War, as well. In Lane's later years, he was the speaker of choice for many religious, philanthropic and patriotic organizations.

Much of Lew Wallace's oration was on a ministry basis. He was appointed minister to Turkey in 1881 and had great influence on the Sultan Abdul Hamid II. When asked why he had had so much influence with the sultan, Wallace responded, "I told him the truth." In fact, when Lew was ready to return to America in 1885, the sultan asked him to stay and accept a post in the Turkish government. Lew declined. One of his lecture tours covered 128 cities. Joan Spragg of the Lew Wallace Study confirmed that he gave lectures in at least 36 states, as well as Canada and Mexico.

The military careers of all three men are surprising. Both Wallace and Lane were adept at creating militia units, but what about their part in the wars? And, how about Abe himself?

Let's begin with Lincoln. Abe (a name he detested; to his friends and colleagues he was "Lincoln") volunteered with the Illinois militia recruited to counter Native American disturbances in what became known as the Black Hawk War. In 1860, he still felt that being elected captain of this company was one of his greatest accomplishments. He reenlisted twice, but never encountered any live Indians. When he mustered out, he received $125 and land in Iowa. Upon his return, he ran a store for a short time, then served as Salem's postmaster and then as a surveyor. Becoming known to a great many people in all these occupations laid the groundwork for his political career.

Lew Wallace's first military experience (at about age 17) came with a militia unit at Indianapolis known as the "Marion Rifles." Lew's father David Wallace had been a cadet at West Point, where in due time he graduated. David Wallace entered the regular army and served three years. He married Esther Test in 1824. Lew was their second son. While not yet 20, during the Mexican War, Lew was a second lieutenant to the First Regiment of Indiana Volunteers, whom he recruited and organized; however, his troops saw little action. In 1856, he recruited a company of men from Montgomery County and called them the "Montgomery Guards." From this unit, Wallace's famous 11th Regiment, the Indiana Zouaves, were created. He held drills several nights a week. He was captain of this group and even wrote their manual of arms.

This image shows a young Lieutenant Lew Wallace. It is one of the earliest known photographs of Wallace.

Lew Wallace was equally famous as an author, Civil War general, lawyer, orator, and painter. He is likely Crawfordsville's best known citizen.

For the Civil War, when Lincoln called for troops, Lew jumped to it. He actually organized the first six regiments from the state of Indiana to serve in the Civil War. Wallace's first choices for troops were the National Guards, City Grays, and Independent Zouaves of Indianapolis; Vigo and Harrison Guards of Terre Haute; and of course, his own Montgomery Guards. In his next round of choices, another Montgomery County group was added, the Ladoga Blues, among others including the Wallace Guards, which he recruited at Camp Morton. All officers and men agreed upon Indiana Zouaves as their name as they used the tactics of the Zouaves. Some of the men complained that there was too great a focus placed on discipline, but Wallace was well-supported by his officers. Oddly, the original uniforms for the Zouaves were gray, but of course were soon changed. An excellent overview of the 11th's part in the Civil War can be gleaned through Joann Spragg's *Montgomery County Magazine* article. According to an article in the second edition of the *Encyclopedia of World Biography*, "as a result of a few very successful maneuvers, he was promoted to Major General, making him the youngest man at that time to hold that rank."

There has been much controversy as to what happened during the Battle of Shiloh on April 6, 1862. Many say that Wallace led his troops to the wrong position, while others say he was misinformed. Wallace certainly took much flack in regards to the problems on the battlefield and was even blamed personally for many losses of lives. In 1864, when his troops successfully held out against a large Confederate force, he redeemed himself by effectively preventing Washington, our nation's capitol, from becoming occupied. It is fitting that one of Lew's last military tasks was to serve on the commission responsible for trying and sentencing those involved in the conspiracy to kill Lincoln. Along this line, he was president of the court martial that tried Henry Wirz, head of the notorious Confederate prison at Andersonville, Georgia. He also served on a "secret service assignment" connected with the liberation of Mexico in 1865, and later (1878–1881) served as governor of the New Mexico Territory.

An interesting tale concerning Billy the Kid occurred while Lew was in this territory. His job was to "clean up the Lincoln County Wars." William Bonny (Billy the Kid) agreed to testify against those involved in the killing of Huston Chapman. He kept his word about testifying, but skipped out before he stood trial. Wallace refused to grant Billy amnesty and, in December 1880, Billy the Kid was again arrested and charged with murdering three men. Although he was only convicted of one death, he was sentenced to hang for this crime and General Lew Wallace's handwriting is on his official death warrant. Of course, Billy escaped again, but was finally shot down by Sheriff Pat Garrett in July 1881.

Lane came by his military aptitude quite naturally just like Wallace. Henry was the son of James H. Lane, a colonel of the militia and a well-known Indian fighter. According to Bowen:

> Henry strongly supported the Mexican War, raised a company of volunteers, became its captain, and subsequently rose to be major, then lieutenant colonel of the 1st Indiana Regiment. He was mainly engaged in guarding supply trains and in garrison duty, and he did not participate in any battles.

Wallace, the youngest of the three men, was born April 10, 1827 in Brookville, Indiana and died February 15, 1905 in Crawfordsville. He, like Lincoln, had a mother who passed away as a young woman. Mainly, he was raised by a stepmother, Zerelda, whom he came to love dearly, just as Lincoln loved his stepmother Sarah Bush. It is assumed that Lane had a normal childhood with both parents.

Another interesting comparison of the three men is their namesake items. Lane had a bank named for him (as he was a partner with his father-in-law) and, of course, Lane Place, as well as Lane Avenue and the Lane House Nursing Home. Lincoln's name is spread throughout the United States, to say nothing of the many products named after him. Although items weren't named so much after Lew Wallace himself, they were indeed named because he wrote the book *Ben-Hur*. Everyone with associations to Crawfordsville knows of the Ben Hur building. Most everyone has gone to a doctor, lawyer, merchant, or chief in the building, and know of the Ben Hur Life Association. Ben Hur Stables and Ben Hur Nursing Home are uppermost in our minds as well. There is also the Ben Hur Tandem Bicycle, Ben Hur March, Ben Hur hairpins, postcards, and the Ben Hur Trail (a touring road that ran from Terre Haute to Huntington, Indiana through Crawfordsville, of course). Also, there was the Ben Hur Metal Polish, Ben Hur Cigars, Ben-Hur Straight Razor, Ben-Hur Chemical Company, Ben-Hur Nutmeg, and the list goes on and on. Thus, Lew Wallace is probably Crawfordsville's most famous man.

Perhaps a bit tacky to mention, yet a point of great interest and definitely something the three men had in common is the fact that none were particularly handsome. The story of Lincoln growing a beard at the suggestion of a young girl (to hide his ugly face) is a very well-known tale; yet, the not so common story of Lincoln's reaction to Lane is rather humorous. Before the Civil War, both Lincoln and Lane were attending court in Fountain County, Indiana when Lane approached a group of men that included Abraham Lincoln. Abe noted, "Here comes an uglier man than I am!" According to research done by Mike Hall, curator of the Lane Place, Lane was "a tall, slim man with a shaky limp, pale complexion, grayish beard, and his cheek was filled with chewing tobacco." Wallace, likely the best looking of the three, was nonetheless no Charleton Heston himself. Wallace at one time described our future president:

> His features were massive, nose long, eyebrows protrusive, mouth large, cheeks hollow, eyes gray and always responsive to humor. He smiled all the time but never once laughed aloud, and he was forever crossing and uncrossing his legs and arms.

Lane's first wife, Pamela Bledso Jameson, died a violent, convulsive death in Henry's arms less than two weeks after being injured in a stagecoach accident. He was extremely happy and very much in love with his second wife Joanna Elston, whom he married three days before Valentine's Day, 1845. According to an article by Jean Thompson,

> Joanna's first public act was to make a speech on June 10, 1846, to present a handmade flag made by the ladies of Crawfordsville to the First Indiana Regiment of Volunteers for Mexico (all Montgomery County men), of which her husband was captain.

She often followed Henry as a campaign volunteer. When Lane was United States senator, she accompanied him to Washington, D.C., where they lived in the National Hotel. Admiral George Brown of the Washington Naval Yard noted, "Mrs. Lane was not only a brilliantly intellectual woman, but one whose character and kindliness made friends of all who met her." She was the sister of General Lew Wallace's wife, Susan Elston.

Both Elston girls, daughters of Colonel Isaac C. Elston, were highly talented, well-educated, and cultured women. All the Elston girls were extremely close. Joanna was just moving a block away as she was preparing to marry Lane; however, she received a touching letter from her elder sister Sylvia:

> Here in our room . . . where we have passed so many days of happiness . . . I am alone . . . as ever my thoughts are of you. Your gentle heart has discovered a new source of happiness, but whatever new ties be formed, let not the silken cord which has so long united us be loosened.

Henry S. Lane, pioneer lawyer, United States senator, and short-time governor of Indiana, was a prominent citizen of Crawfordsville. His home, Lane Place, houses the Montgomery County Historical Society.

Their mother was one of the five charter members of First Methodist Church of Crawfordsville. Isaac Elston was one of the founders of Asbury (now DePauw University). Henry S. Lane was a trustee of the college for many years, and Mrs. Lane continued with financial support to the college after her husband's death. Although Joanna Lane possessed an avid interest in music, art, literature, writing, religion, and politics, she was adverse to the "new woman" of her day. She always believed that woman's highest glory was attained through home-making, probably the reason the Lane Place was indeed one of the most popular spots in Crawfordsville.

Susan Elston Wallace was an impressive writer in her own right. She authored six books and numerous magazine and newspaper articles. Possibly her most noteworthy accomplishment was written with another of Crawfordsville's famous authors, Mary Hannah Krout. This was the completion of Lew's autobiography that he had started before his death. The Wallaces were deeply in love and many letters between the two show this fact. Fifty years after their marriage, he called her "a composite of genius, commonsense and all best womanly qualities." One of the best historical spots in Montgomery County, Indiana is the Lew Wallace Study, found on Wallace Avenue and Pike Streets, Crawfordsville. In the *Dictionary of American Biography*, we find this quote in regards to the study: "Many a young person had reason to remember the gracious hospitality of his study." The study is where Lew wrote most of *Ben-Hur*. It was noted that Lew was more of a romantic, while his wife was much more practical. Pertaining to their long marriage, Wallace wrote, "She held my hand in defeat, and rejoiced in my triumphs, but boy could she scold!"

Now we come to Mrs. Lincoln. Mary Todd Lincoln and the Elston sisters all had several things in common. Number one was their love for their husbands. Number two was the undying faith regarding their husbands' abilities to succeed in large scale. Mary was said to have been "vivacious, impulsive, interesting, witty, and sarcastic." According to the White House first ladies web page, "All of these attributes marked her life, bringing her happiness and tragedy." She, like the Elstons, was a highly intelligent woman with a "sound private education." Mary met Lincoln when she went to Springfield to visit her sister. In the Newbery award-winning book *Lincoln: A Photobiography*, Mary is described as being "the very creature of excitement." Mary's sister and brother-in-law considered Lincoln a "very rough man." Abe and Mary had a "tumultuous relationship, including a broken engagement, yet Abraham Lincoln and Mary Todd were finally united in marriage."

Always one for finery, Mary kept Abe hopping in order to keep her and their boys "kept." Her faith in her husband was confirmed with his 1860 election as president. She soon spent much money, which caused more comment. In fact, she seemed never to win with the public. When she held galas, she was accused of extravagance. Yet when she curtailed her entertaining after her son Willie's death in 1862, she was said to be shirking her social duties. Nothing affected the love Abe felt for the woman, however. He told his guests in the White House, "My wife is as handsome as when she was a girl, and I . . . fell in love with her;

This old postcard depicts Ben Hur, *the book by Lew Wallace that was made into a well-loved film.*

and what is more, I have never fallen out." Lincoln always referred to Mary as Mother and she referred to him as Father. Mary's life was actually one of much tragedy—losing a mother, all but one of her children, and her beloved spouse—so it was fitting that she passed away at her sister's home in Springfield, the same house where 40 years before she had walked as the bride of Abe Lincoln.

There is one last likeness to consider: that of their funerals. Lincoln, as is widely known, lay in state for all of Washington, D.C. to "see" after which his body was taken by train to Springfield, Illinois. It made several stops along the way for his folks to pay respects. The funeral train followed the same route that Lincoln had taken when he went to Washington, D.C. as president. Soldiers and citizens waited for hours to view the body. A military band played, bells tolled, and guns fired salute. "As president, he had been denounced, ridiculed and damned by a legion of critics, but as the slain President Abraham Lincoln, he was revered!" It is controversial whether Lincoln's funeral train came through Crawfordsville on the Monon track, but it is said that Wallace wrote a portion of *Ben-Hur* while riding on the Monon.

For Lew Wallace, it was similar. Flags were at half mast, businesses closed, his body lay in state, and there were full military rites. Also, as with Lincoln, "all kinds of society were represented for General Wallace was democratic to the core, and held in high esteem of all classes," according to his obituary. Wallace's massive black casket sat on the spot where most of his later writing was done.

Many dignitaries took part in Lane's funeral, including Governor Albert Porter, Senators Benjamin Harrison and Dan Vorhees, ex-governor Hendricks, Professor John Campbell, and Wabash College president Joseph Tuttle. His coffin was opened on the lawn of Lane Place and his peaceful face was viewed by thousands of people. His funeral procession, like Lew's and Lincoln's, was large and consisted of hundreds of assorted vehicles. The Odd Fellows organization had charge of his funeral. It is safe to say that all three men were highly loved by their peers and fellow community members.

The differences of the three men now need to be addressed. Lew Wallace was quite the creative one. His painting was outstanding. He held United States patents for several railroad inventions, including railroad ties and couplers. Also, he invented an apparatus for molding blocks for fence posts and a fishing rod (he loved to fish). A Canadian patent was held for railway ties and he had an English one for several improvements to railway ties, sleeper joints, and fastening devices. Wallace also had several books to his name, not just his famous *Ben-Hur*.

According to Mike Hall, curator of the Lane Place, "Lane did not invent anything tangible, but when he was in the Senate he was a big advocate of designing irrigation projects that would allow the great western Plains to be farmed." Everyone hooted at the idea of anyone desiring to live there, but once the railroads went west, people began going west, too. Hall said, "By some fluke, the wettest years ever recorded on the Plains fell between 1871 and 1881. After the climate returned to normal, many farms failed. That was . . . until irrigation projects started years later, just like Lane had proposed way back in 1863."

Lincoln, of course, grew up in rural Kentucky, Indiana and later lived in the back area of Illinois. His father Thomas was a poor farmer, having had troubles with land disputes in Kentucky when Abe was a boy. Abe's mother Nancy Hanks died when the boy was nine. This was a hard blow to the young man and he would not accept her death until a traveling preacher finally spoke a real funeral for the woman. Abe loved his stepmother Sarah Bush Johnston. It is thought that it was she of whom he spoke this thought, "God bless my mother; all that I am or ever hope to be, I owe to her." Lincoln's physical labor as a wood chopper, his prowess as a hiker, his strength in plowing a field or rowing a boat are all known to the majority of American history buffs. The Lincolns were of course the parents of Robert Todd Lincoln (the only one of their sons to reach maturity), Edward Baker Lincoln (who died at age four), William (Willie) Wallace Lincoln (who died while Lincoln was president), and Thomas Lincoln (named for Lincoln's father and called "Tad," who died at age 18.) The Wallaces were the parents of one son, appropriately named Henry Lane Wallace. The Lanes, on the other hand, never had children, but were quite indulgent, often helping with the educational endeavors of young folk.

Abraham Lincoln had ties to Crawfordsville. Henry S. Lane nominated Lincoln for President and Lew Wallace headed the trial of the conspirators who killed him.

5. "Our Colored People"

Always an intricate and integrated part of our community, there were a few shy of 100 African Americans living in Montgomery County in 1850. The majority were in Crawfordsville. Oddly, just three short years later when all African Americans were required to register or be sent back to the South, there were only 61. The following was in the Crawfordsville papers at this time:

> NOTICE: Is hereby given that all Negroes and Mulattoes who were inhabitants of the State of Indiana, prior to the first day of November, A.D. 1851, and entitled to reside therein, are required to appear before the clerk of the Circuit Court for registry.

The larger families coming to register were the Higgins, Johnson, Jones, Kerns, Ketchums, Luthers, Pattersons, Smiths, Williams, and Wilsons. A typical description of a person in the Register of Negro & Mulattoes is:

> Mary Petifor, aged about 18 years, a Negro woman, light brown color, about 5' high, born in the state of Indiana, residence of Crawfordsville, Indiana on the 15th day of August A.D. 1853 for registry and it was proved to the satisfaction of said Clerk by the testimony of William S. Galey, that said Mary Petifor was an inhabitant of the state of Indiana at and prior to the first day of November A.D. 1851. Therefore, it is determined by said Clerk that said Mary Petifor is entitled to reside in the state of Indiana. Registered August 15, A.D. 1853.

Dr. Israel Thompson Canby, an early Crawfordsville settler, had several African-American servants. He provided homes for them and they were freed peoples. One of them, Mrs. Cassy Ketchum, was of high intelligence and sterling character. She was more than 100 years old when she died. According to an article by Mary Hannah Krout, "Cassy had lived as a child in Baltimore, and used to describe the evacuation of the city by the British, which she witnessed in the War of 1812."

In Frank Mills's fabulous Crawfordsville history, which he wrote when he was past 90, he stated, "The colored population was not very great. Old Judge Peter

Smith was an aristocratic old barber who had great pride." Jim Askins was Frank's favorite barber. He got his first shave from "Old Jim," who kept his customer accounts by marking on his wall, each person having a special place.

One of Crawfordsville's early prominent African Americans was Robert S. Jones, who was born a freeman September 2, 1818 in Butler County, Ohio, although his father John was a slave until age 22. Robert's mother Dorothy Sampson was also born a slave, but she, like Robert's father, was freed by a master. Robert's parents moved to Montgomery County, Indiana about 1840 and bought 6 acres a mile east of Crawfordsville. They died here in the 1850s. Robert attended school to sufficiently enable him to read, write, and cipher. He prized that small amount of learning. Robert married Dilly Henderson in Ohio in 1836. She too had been a slave.

The Robert Jones family rented 80 acres west of Crawfordsville for several years before finally buying 40 acres in Walnut Township. Robert's first wife died in 1842. He then married Susan McKee of Crawfordsville. Together, Robert and Susan had at least eight children. A Mason, a warm Republican, and a lover of Lincoln, Robert Jones's major contribution would probably be that he was a member of the first African Methodist Episcopal (AME) class in Montgomery County and was said to have contributed the first timber toward the church. He was a trustee for almost 30 years.

According to research by Martha Cantrell, Montgomery County had 15 Underground Railroad depots. John Speed's family, mentioned earlier, encouraged members of the AME Church to help slaves to freedom. Members of Wabash faculty aided, as well as Jesse Cumberland (a buggy maker), who married one of Speed's daughters. Several doctors, with enclosed buggies and health-related night journeys, helped transport slaves to other stations. These doctors were Joseph Emmons and Iral and Ryland T. Brown.

Montgomery County sent 16 African-American soldiers to the Civil War. A list was compiled by Keith Houk and can be found in *Family Histories of Montgomery County*.

During the late 1880s and beyond, an "Our Colored People" section appeared in the local papers. Tidbits such as "Thomas May went to Danville, Illinois yesterday to attend the bedside of his child" were found there.

In 1881, an order created an African-American school on the southwest corner of Spring and North Walnut Streets. This became known as Lincoln School. The decision was not so much a racial question as one of overcrowding, as most of the African-American families lived in the area where the school was built. The school had no windows on the front and only a few on the back, but to some it was noted as a fine school. By 1922, the population was shifting and more whites were moving into the north part of the city, while blacks were moving east, thus a new Lincoln School was built on East Wabash. Students through the eighth grade attended the school for several years, but finally blacks and whites went to neighborhood schools. Lincoln School was used for Masonic meetings and by the Baptist church for a short time before it was torn down in 1981.

A January 1988 *Montgomery* article tells of a little known fact regarding Crawfordsville baseball and an early black player. In 1888, baseball was the number one sport in Crawfordsville. Even the *Indianapolis Press* commented:

> There is but one thing that will draw the average Crawfordsville citizen from the pleasures of verse or fiction making. That is baseball! Baseball as played in Crawfordsville is not only a science; it is a passion, deep-seated and permeating every branch of society.

Even Professors Campbell and Coulter dismissed afternoon classes because of sickness, yet would be seen at the local baseball park. Lew Wallace watched the games when he was in town and sometimes could be seen playing in the neighborhood. The article ended by asking, "Thus do the twin arts of baseball and literature go hand in hand in the Athens of Indiana?"

On June 2, 1988, the local paper stated "that it was no dishonor to be defeated in a well-played game, but such a rout as the Hoosiers received yesterday is to be deplored." They even suspended the third baseman, Barnes, because he had been on a "two nights debauch in Indianapolis. Crawfordsville has no use for him." It was evidently a cut-throat game, but John "Bud" Fowler (John W. Jackson) was up to it. He played second base for Crawfordsville. Fowler started his career with a white team in New Castle, Pennsylvania and was said to have been the first black player to do so. Fowler could play any position, but he was fantastic as a second baseman.

Born in Fort Plain, New York on March 16, 1858, he was about 30 when he played for the Crawfordsville team. At one point, he was fined $50 because he

The Lincoln School for African Americans was located on the southwest corner of Spring and North Walnut.

Wilbur de Paris, a Crawfordsville citizen, played trumpet with several famous early jazz bands.

would not catch a white player who would not take signals from him. An 1885 Denver paper stated Fowler had two strong points: that he was an excellent runner and that he didn't get a sunburn. In one Crawfordsville game in 1888, he played his famous position of second with eight put-outs, seven assists, and only one error. Another paper commented about his five steals and felt that if they could paint him white, he'd be playing in much better leagues. His career batting average was .337 and although he didn't play for Crawfordsville long, we were lucky to have him!

Born in 1900 in the city, Wilbur de Paris heard his first jazz at age 12 when he was a member of his father's summer traveling show. He played the slide trombone and his brother Sidney played the cornet. Omer Simeon, clarinetist, was the other member of a New York 52nd Street band for many years. Wilbur even played with Louis Armstrong! The de Paris boys began playing so early they could hardly hold up their instruments. *Marchin' and Swingin'* and *New Orleans Blues* are two of their albums. Both are unique jazz experiences.

In 1902, Crawfordsville graduated 20 pupils, three of whom (Timothy Davis, Eva Johnson, and Blanche Patterson) were African Americans. Blanche never married, was an active member of the AME Church, where she was a pianist, and also belonged to the Missionary Society. Her cello playing was considered outstanding. She went on from CHS to complete a course at Wilberforce University in Xenia, Ohio.

In 1922, Blanche served as state chairman of the Federation of Colored Women. She served as secretary for many years of the local NAACP. In 1982, according to an article written by John Bowerman, Blanche's piano was housed in the little church that she loved so well. Blanche took care of the ladies of Crawfordsville from head to toe as an active podiatrist, as well as a beautician. Oddly, it was said that she only did white folks' hair. Her office was in the Ben Hur Building. One icy winter day, "Miss Blanche" was on her way to see a hospitalized friend when she was hit by a truck. She died from multiple injuries at the age of 80, having been born here to George Frank and Sarah Belle Keene Patterson on August 9, 1884.

About the time Blanche was graduating from high school, Samuel S. Gordon was playing football for Wabash College. The young Gordon joined Blanche as an active member in the local black church. The president of Wabash at this time was William Kane and the football coach was Tug Wilson. What was unusual in regards to Gordon is that football was indeed a segregated sport at this time. Hanover College "notified Wabash that if Gordon were on the team, it would

Blanche Patterson, Crawfordsville High School graduate of 1902, returned to the city after graduating from college. She became quite an active worker in the local African-American church and the community, and was highly respected.

cancel the October 24th game." Wabash's teammates loved Gordon and backed him all the way. Gordon told Coach Wilson that he wished to play and the chapel roared with applause as Wilson stated he could. Next, DePauw officials refused! A delegation of five Methodist ministers pleaded with the team to not bring disgrace upon DePauw, but it took General Lew Wallace to influence DePauw otherwise, and finally the game began; Wabash won 10 to 0. The Wabash team at this time was called "Little Men," and the little men were "giants" among the best as they rallied around Samuel S. Gordon. Gordon served in World War I and later became superintendent of the West Virginia Industrial School for Colored Boys.

In 1916, the Lincoln School students put on an unforgettable music performance under the leadership of Blanche Woody. Professor Hines, chairman of the Montgomery County Centennial Committee, was so impressed with the fine voices that he asked that the children be put on the centennial program. Eleven children graduated that year from the eighth grade. George W. Thompson, principal, told his students that opportunities were never better for the African American whose conduct is above reproach and who proves himself to his community.

Thus was the case for one well-loved woman, Frances Wooden. John Bowerman stated the following:

> The greatness and strength of any community is determined by the moral attributes of those who make up the land in which we live . . . unsung heroes transform the lives of the youth. In Crawfordsville, Frances was one of these heroes, and increasingly, with the passing of time, her life becomes a profile of inspiration.

For several years, her mother Fanny was in charge of the kitchen at the Phi Gamma Delta Fraternity at Wabash College and Frances's father Elijah worked odd jobs. The Wooden family lived on Beech Street in Crawfordsville.

A 1935 graduate of CHS, Frances loved music. It became her solace, especially after developing polio. Her effort to receive that coveted diploma was a major task with her disability. Very religious, she read her Bible daily. Under her graduation picture was the legend, "Great works are performed by perseverance." She even found a job working for the Welfare Department at the old YMCA building at the corner of Pike and Green. Her favorite Bible passage read, "Let the children come to me, do not hinder them; for to such belongs the kingdom of God."

The children did indeed come and Rita Hamm, longtime director of the Park and Recreation Department, said that Frances was a pioneer. She organized cooking and sewing classes for mothers, as well as for the youngsters themselves. She taught the Northside children to be proud of their area and to keep it clean. Youngsters who were too poor to buy needed supplies to make crafts were never excluded. Retiring December 30, 1982, she had worked with children for more than 35 years. On June 7, 1985, Mayor Glenn Knecht headed a Frances Wooden Day, appropriately held in the Northside Recreation Center where she had spent so many years with her beloved children. It wasn't just the mayor

This 506 West Wabash structure was home to the men of Delta Tau Delta Fraternity at Wabash College for quite some time before they built their current house across the street.

and the Crawfordsville folks who thought she deserved recognition, however, as Governor Robert Orr also recognized her with a Special Appreciation Award for her many years of dedication as a public employee; "She felt the hand of her Precious Lord leading her home on January 20, 1987."

Janet Lambert, a local writer, noted what she felt was the first hint of racism in the town. "There was to be a Flower Parade and the Keane girls—Blanche and Belle [possibly Blanche and Belle Patterson, whose mother was a Keane] had entered a horse and carriage." Some of the white populace threatened to withdraw their entries. Janet's father was the parade marshal and he solved the problem in a rather unique way:

> He told them that since he was sure that they could decorate a carriage and win hands down, he would like to give them the first prize money and save them the expense of doing so. They were happy with the fifty dollars he paid them out of his own pocket and the town folk were satisfied, too.

Ronny Rankin was the first African-American man to work in a plant, R.R. Donnelleys. Ruby and Leslie Dean were the first blacks to build a house (on East Wabash). Andy Robinson has been the mentor and friend of many children, black and white. A volunteer at the Boys and Girls Club for decades and a current board member, Andy played ping pong and counseled many Crawfordsville youths. His lovely wife Jasmine recently retired from Wabash College after working there for many years as an administrative assistant for the Computer Center. The Bill Lee family has been residents of Crawfordsville for several decades. Bill is a minister and raised his superbly musically-inclined family of 12 here.

Speaking of church, the AME Church has played an intricate part in the lives of many African Americans in our city for decades. The Bethel AME here in Crawfordsville was one of the first congregations of free blacks in a large radius. The first church (on the same site) was a log cabin, built about 1847. Van Tapp, who worked in the Ben Hur Building for 45 years, was a faithful member, as was his wife Bertha, daughter of Reverend Charles Brown, the minister. Reverend Brown had a barbershop in his home, too. The Baptist church has also been important, dating back 130 years.

In the 1950s, there were about 200 blacks in the city. Crawfordsville has always been proud of her African-American population. However, as just about everywhere else, in the 1960s there was strife among the blacks and whites. Restaurants, hotels, and other public buildings did not allow blacks in. Also, African-American children were made to drink from separate fountains in school. This prompted a poll, taken by a committee of concerned white citizens, of businesses in the area serving blacks. There was only one barber in Crawfordsville who would cut African Americans' hair. A white woman took her son there. While the barber was cutting her son's hair, she mentioned to the barber how proud she was of him allowing blacks into his shop. He said, "Well, I had so much pressure from so many people that I've changed my mind about that." The woman promptly and proudly jerked her son out of the barber's chair and took him home with his hair half cut!

The Bethel African American Episcopal Church (AME) has been important to African-American history in Crawfordsville for many decades.

6. Crawfordsville's Businesses

It would take multiple volumes to include all the businesses to ever have existed in Crawfordsville, but many of the long-standing ones will be discussed here.

Fittingly, one of our finest citizens, Major Isaac C. Elston, began what was one of Montgomery County's ultimate businesses. Born on October 8, 1794, Elston was not a particularly young man when he started the banking business in Crawfordsville. He had one of the first trading posts in the infant town as early as 1823. He traded with the Native Americans as well as the white men and was equally honest on both counts. Elston married Maria E. Aiken and had nine children, one of whom, Isaac C. Elston Jr., followed in his father's footsteps.

In 1852, Indiana established the First and Second Bank of Indiana, which allowed individuals to own and finance private banks. The following year, Major Elston set up the first financial institution in Crawfordsville. Soon after, Elston took his son-in-law Henry S. Lane into business under the new name Elston-Lane. Still later, another son-in-law, Lew Wallace, became a member and it was then called Elston & Company. Twelve years after the establishment of Elston's firm, the First National Bank of Crawfordsville came on the scene, followed in 1880 by the Citizens National Bank. In 1900, the Elston firm became known as the Elston National Bank. Under the major's son, I.C. Elston, the bank flourished and, in 1925, the Elstons acquired two other Crawfordsville banks, the Farmers-Merchants and Clements Trust. Immediately thereafter, it took out a state banking charter that permitted state banks to do trust business and took on the name most Montgomery Countians of today remember: the Elston Bank & Trust Company.

Other similar businesses in this time were the Crawfordsville Trust Company, the Union Trust Company, and the Crawfordsville State Bank. Elston had ventured into Crawfordsville in October 1824, bringing his wife Maria and baby Sylvia. He felled trees to erect his first home, somewhat south of the center of town at that point. The Elston family grew and, within ten years, it was obvious that the major needed a new home for his brood. Thus, in August 1834, the Elstons hired carpenter Thornton Griffith to build their new home in what would become familiarly known as "Elston Grove." Griffith was paid $1.50 per day. The new dwelling, a Federalist design, would come to have 15 panel doors, and both poplar and ash flooring.

Farmer's Merchant and Clements Trust were owned by the Elston family. The Elston name is seen throughout Indiana, one example being Isaac C. Elston High School in Michigan City.

More than a year later, in December 1835, the Elstons moved with their five children into the new home. Besides the banking business, Elston was a storekeeper, postmaster, and very large land developer. He was the largest contributor to the Methodist Episcopal Church building fund. Several of the Elston children lived within walking distance of the homestead: Mary Elston and her husband Hector Braden; Joanna Elston and her husband Henry S. Lane; Susan Elston and Lew Wallace; Helen Elston and Aaron Blair; and the Isaac Elston Jr. family. More can be read about this family in *The Quilt Chronicles*.

Montgomery Savings Association is over 110 years old, getting its start in July 1888. It recently merged with Union Federal. William Ireland was elected the president of the board for the establishment, while J.W. Cumberland was elected vice president; A.C. Jennison, secretary; and George Robinson, treasurer. Other directors were Hume DeBrular, Carl Rost, and E.G. Wilson. The *Crawfordsville Journal* noted that persons desiring stock ($100 a share) could get it from the directors. The association started at 113 North Washington Street. The first loan approved was for $700 (at 6 percent yearly interest). By June 1889, there were so many loans being requested that the officers decided to borrow $2,500 from Citizens Bank to accommodate its applicants. Some of the facility's board presidents have been Judge Jere West, Sol Tannenbaum (whom Crawfordsville owes a great debt for his philanthropic donations), William Sprow (former Crawfordsville mayor), Earl Berry, Ralph Bounnell, Richard Huseman, and Earl Elliott. The goal for the association was "Not to be a bank, but to be a savings and mortgage lending firm." The Crawford Hotel was one of Montgomery Savings' homes for awhile, as well as 119 East Main Street.

An interesting note found in Herbert C. Morrison's chapter in *Montgomery County Remembers* is that when President Franklin D. Roosevelt closed the banks to reopen them after an examination of their finances, every bank in Montgomery County got an "A." Today's banking firms are somewhat different than the original ones that had businessmen as bank officers, but Bank One, Farmers State Bank, Indiana Community Bank, Lincoln Federal Savings, National City, Tri-County Bank & Trust, and Union Federal Savings & Loan continue giving Crawfordsvillians fine service.

Although the Crawfordsville Airport isn't in town, it is a big part of our town's history. In April 1945, a two-seat, yellow plane landed, the first plane to land at the newly established Crawfordsville Airport. A sad note in relation to the airport occurred not long after it opened when the hangars and 19 planes were destroyed by a tornado. Dorothy Hill, wife of Chet Hill, the airport's first flight instructor

Isaac C. Elston created one of the largest businesses in Crawfordsville. Family members carried on the banking dynasty for decades to come.

and manager, wrote a wonderful article in *Montgomery County Remembers* regarding the airport. Its main ideas will be highlighted here.

The Hills lived in the old farmhouse on the airport property so that there would be someone there at all times. Although there was no indoor plumbing or electricity when the Hills moved in, they loved their work and mostly ignored the inconveniences. Many World War II returning soldiers desired to learn to fly and, with the GI Program, the airport needed a shop and mechanic. Dr. Thomas Cooksey, then mayor of Crawfordsville, appointed an aviation commission to operate and manage the airport. The first members were Raymond O. Evans, Lex Clore, Herrick Grossman, and Thomas Luster.

Interesting early happenings included a "Field Day," when over 100 farmers took rides in eight different planes in order to see their farms from the air. The Montgomery County Home Economic Chorus served lunch and 22 dealers in farm implements had equipment and displays for over 500 attendees. Dorothy noted that in one of her monthly reports to the city, there were 111 solo students. O.K. Galloway's new automobile sales had one of Crawfordsville's new Cessna airplanes for its open house, and Chet took a 100-year-old lady for her first and only ride on her birthday. Some famous folks who landed at the airport have been Bill Piper (airplane manufacturer), Wilbur Shaw (of Indianapolis 500 fame), Robert Redford, and Robert Kennedy.

For several years, a small drive-in served the many folks who watched the planes at the Crawfordsville Airport for entertainment. Although the airport saw many exciting happenings, Crawfordsville's actual first landing of a plane occurred many years before the airport came to exist. On May 25, 1918, Louis Spilman, a new pilot in the United States Army Signal Corps, landed in a field where the Crawfordsville Square Shopping Center is today. A mechanic accompanied him on the flight from the Speedway grounds to Crawfordsville, letting the active interurban tracks guide him to his hometown. Railroad agents phoned Spilman's progress. When he reached the Crawfordsville area, he dropped a couple hundred leaflets explaining war bonds over the city. A few aerial antics by the 19-year-old aviator made the mechanic sick. Spilman took his father Theodore Bruce Spilman for a ride, as well as his fiancee Emily Moon and Crawfordsville businessman Ed Vorhies before returning the plane to Indianapolis. This was tagged as the first "air" mail for the city.

Crawfordsville Wire and Nail supplied farmers fencing and builders nails, among other wire items. Founded a few days before Christmas in 1900, William P. Herron was its first president with Dr. Irwin Detchon, vice president, and secretary-treasurer Clifford D. Voris. Twenty-eight years later, the Keystone Steel and Wire Company of Peoria, Illinois made a mid-states division. Jon Sommer, inventor of a machine to manufacture wire fencing, became its first president. Edwin Sommer, son of John, served as Mid-State's head for many years. In 1968, the company became Keystone Consolidated Industries and later became Mid-States Wire. One of the products produced was florist wire. In 1984, the plant employed 350 with an annual payroll of $7 million. A number of

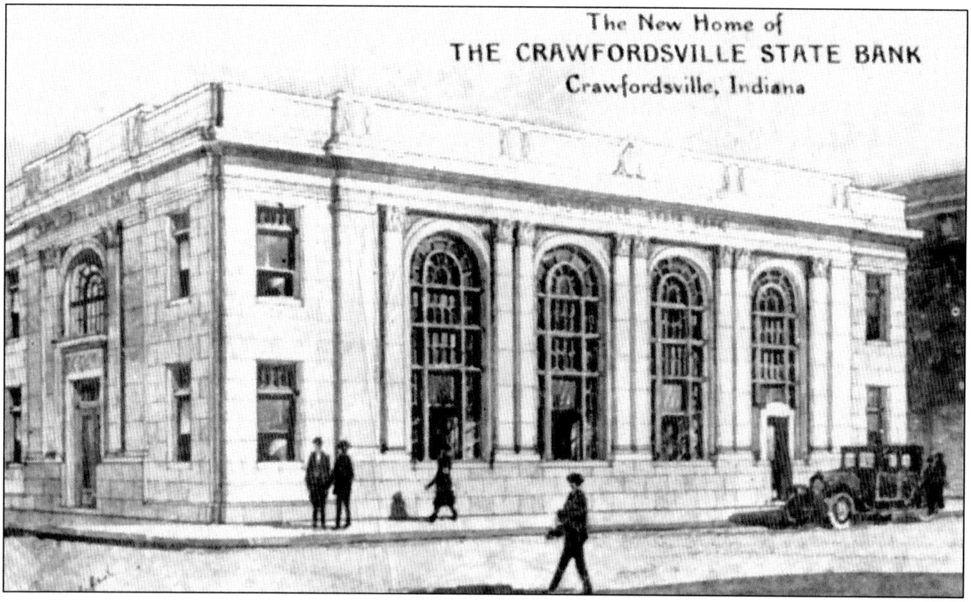

The Crawfordsville State Bank was purchased by the Elston family as well and served the community for many years.

second- and third-generation employees worked at the plant. Sadly, Mid-States closed its doors on November 22, 1998. Luckily, Crawfordsville still has Sommer Metalcraft on Poston Road, a local employer for several decades.

Located in a brick building on Elmore Street, the Federal Match Factory employed many in our area in the early 1900s. In 1917, a woman assigned to the head of a machine made $3.50 per day, the second woman $1 less, and the third $1 less than the second. The person at the foot of the machine made $1 even; however, the majority of the employees at this time made only 15¢ per hour.

Part of the whole "Athens" idea is music and the Lyons Music Company was a part of Crawfordsville for more than three-quarters of a century. According to an article by Don Thompson, the music establishment first began on May 1, 1915 with just "one new piano, one used one, a phonograph, some records and a few musical accessories." The owner was Leslie Lyons, whose wife had a small hat shop in the store for some time as well. Leslie was born on May 1, 1883 at Gosport. He left the high school there just short of graduation so that he could join the "Gentry Brothers Circus Band." In the 1930s, a saxophone/piano ensemble was formed and they played in many local affairs, including 32 commencements in one year. Lyons was instrumental in getting area schools to use the Conn tonette, "a small instrument that sold for one dollar and which could be used for grade school children to see if they had any musical aptitude," according to Thompson. Besides music, other interests of Lyons included raising Shetland ponies, one of which sold for $20,000. He and his wife Leona were active members of St. John's Church.

One of Crawfordsville's longstanding jewelry companies opened in the fall of 1932 when Edwin K. Resoner came to town for the specific reason of opening his store, after having been a jeweler in Muncie for a number of years. The new store was on 106 South Green Street, but because of a disastrous fire on January 10, 1933 that was too close for comfort (just across the street), the Resoners decided to move their business to a rented building at 128 East Main Street. In 1936, the Resoners bought this building and the August 8, 1936 *Journal* saw this purchase as an "Indication of the increasing commercial expansion and business improvement." E.K. and his wife Helen did extensive remodeling to the store about this time. One item in particular that attracted great attention was a large, "fire-proof, burglar-proof vault which offered patrons the benefit of absolute safety in store of valuables left for repairs," again according to Thompson. E.K. Resoner didn't only move to Crawfordsville to open a business. He was an active member of the community as well. Rotary, Elks, Eagles, Indiana Jewelers, and St. John's Church were among some of his affiliations. The store closed about 1995. Hinesley's was run by a Hinesley for several decades. In 1960, Resoner's moved to the corner of Washington and Main. At some point in the 1990s, Jerry Hupp bought into the store and it became known as Hupp-Resoner.

Another highly respected and longtime Crawfordsville jeweler was Leonard Winchell. Leonard, a country boy, met city girl Louise Weeks. He told her that he was going to own a jewelry store someday. This was 1942, shortly after World War II began. At the time, Louise was working as a secretary during the day and taking an accounting course in the evening. Leonard said that every jewelry store needed a bookkeeper. Louise said she must have applied for the job then and there, as she

Leonard and Louise Winchell's first jewelry store—Winchell's Jewelry—was located in the Ben Hur Building in Room 504 from 1950 to 1955.

got it! The Winchells met at a dance in Chicago shortly after Leonard joined the Navy in February 1942. After basic training at Great Lakes, Leonard was sent to Navy Pier in Chicago for aviation mechanic training. In November 1942, he was sent to Pearl Harbor, Hawaii where he remained until the war was over. Because he was a watchmaker, he was assigned to the instrument shop where the fighter planes for the Pacific Fleet were commissioned.

Born in Ashton, Iowa on September 5, 1915, Leonard was the son of Louis and Anna (Seivert) Winchell. Leonard graduated from St. Joseph High School in 1933. Ashton, a small town of 600, had a large Catholic High School staffed by 13 nuns. After graduation and a few months in the Civilian Conservation Corps, Leonard went to work for the Iowa Highway Commission. A coworker showed him a pamphlet on the Elgin Watchmakers College in Illinois. This is something he thought he wanted to do. After 15 months of training, Frank Marter from Crawfordsville came to Elgin looking for a watchmaker. He met with Leonard and Leonard accepted his job offer. The Marters had been in the jewelry business since 1933. Leonard worked for Marter for a year, returning to work for him after the Navy. Leonard rented a room at Countess Tinsley's home on the southwest corner of Pike and Grant. It cost him $2.50 a week.

In February 1947, Leonard and Louise were married in Chicago and moved into an apartment at 511 East Wabash, owned by the U.G. Vails. The Vails formerly managed the old Ramsey Hotel on the northwest corner of Market and Green. This was later torn down to make room for the Elston Bank drive-through and is now the location of the CVS Pharmacy. After working for the Marters for a few more years, Leonard and Louise got the itch to have their own store. There wasn't much available as far as shop space, so in March 1950, they located to Room 504 in the Ben Hur Building. Also, Louise put her bookkeeping practice to work at Union Savings from 1950 to 1958. Their new store started with a watchmaker's bench, watch material supplies, a hand-operated cleaning machine, and one showcase for the jewelry. Rent, heat, and janitorial service was only $37.50 a month. Van Tapp and Russell Anderson kept the place spotless. The Winchells added two more showcases and jewelry, but desired a store "on the street." Finally, in 1955, a store at 103 North Green was found to rent. This was the old Burke Barber Shop, located behind the Elston Bank Building. The store required a lot of remodeling, but they were excited and happy to be on the street.

The building was later purchased by the Elston Bank. In 1959, the bank needed more room and asked the Winchells to move next door to 105 North Green. That year brought not only a new store, but a new employee as well. Hubert Danzebrink, a native of Duisburg, Germany, had come to Lafayette, Indiana to visit his uncle, also a watchmaker. Watchmakers knowing English could make more money in Germany and that was Hubert's original plan. One evening at a dinner meeting in Lafayette in November 1955, Hubert and Leonard met. Leonard hired Hubert the very next day. Hubert was an expert watchmaker, having worked in Germany and Switzerland before coming to the United States. Leonard said, "In 40 years of working together, we never had words!" Hubert's

Shaw's Meats was one of Crawfordsville's flourishing businesses in the mid-1900s. Started by William A. Shaw, the business was passed down to son Pressley, then to his son. The original location was the north side of West Main, later moving to the old Terminal building on the south side of West Main. The business closed in 1961.

father told him that he should become a citizen if he was staying here; Hubert did as soon as possible.

In 1960, he met a girl. Several women (including Louise) were working on getting Dorothy Kohl fixed up with the nice young man who worked for the Winchells. Dorothy had heard that he was a "big fellow with red hair," and wasn't particularly looking forward to it, but they were married one year later in October 1961. Hubert's parents were visiting Crawfordsville that summer and, of course, stayed for the wedding. The Winchells are like grandparents to the three Danzebrink children (and their children).

In 1971, Winchell's Jewelers made more changes. Leonard sold half interest to Hubert and again they moved. This time it was to the present location at 109 North Washington Street. The Winchells bought this building. It took thousands of dollars to remodel, but it was well worth it. The highlight of many a visit to the store is the beautifully restored (by Hubert) courthouse tower clock, displayed on a balcony overlooking the store. In 1998, Hubert and Leonard decided to retire. Hubert was 65 and Leonard 83. They sold the store to John Owens. John and his family are getting to know Crawfordsville and Crawfordsvillians are glad that Winchell's is still part of downtown. When Leonard was asked if he missed it, he quickly shouted, "No!" But he just as quickly shouted, "Yes!" to the question, "Did you make the right decision to be in the jewelry business?" Leonard and Louise enjoy traveling, as well as their clubs and garden. Another love of both is their church.

Caterers come and go and we can all name a few, but the one who stands out in current Crawfordsvillians' minds is Doris Remley. She spent 50 years feeding Montgomery County folks. Doris always loved to cook and began her career at the request of relatives to prepare Christmas dinner for ten. It didn't take long before she was preparing meals for hundreds. It took a week to prepare for the Farm Progress Show banquet of 1,000 people. In 1976, Doris even flew to California to cater a dinner for 12 for Bill and Ginny Hays. Any banquet-goer of our area can attest that Doris ranks among the best cooks ever!

Speaking of cooking, who remembers coney days at Zach's Family Restaurant or going farther back, the A&W or B-K? All three were establishments of the Zach family. Bill and JoAn Zach purchased two drive-ins in 1955. The Toot 'n Tell was located on the point of East Main Street and Traction Road. The B-K was on Greencastle Road across from today's Dairy Queen. Few employees were needed other than carhops, who made 35¢ an hour. A new A&W took the place of the Toot 'n Tell in 1961. In 1966, land across from the south opening of the recently built Boulevard Mall was purchased, the B-K franchise terminated, and the new A&W built. Opening date was not until National Root Beer Week in September 1967. Inside seating accommodated 50 and electric ordering was provided for 32 cars. At that time, the entire Zach family worked—Bill as owner/manager, JoAn as bookkeeper, son Jim as assistant manager, and daughters Barb and Becky as counter waitresses. It was an elite A&W and one of many Crawfordsvillians' fondest memories was the 19¢ coneys in 1969.

That year, an addition boosted seating to 90. In late 1971, the pagoda roof was added and the seating topped off at 115. In 1972, Bill was president of the Indiana A&W Association. The cash register system was computerized the next year and 43 employees tallied hours. Another famous dish, biscuits and gravy (made by

The A&W, before the Pagoda Roof was added, was famous for "Coney Day" and root beer. Members of the Zach family were in the restaurant business in Crawfordsville for more than 40 years.

longtime head cook Margaret McKinney), was added with the newly-created breakfast menu. In 1980, A&W was dropped and Zach's Family Restaurant became a household name. Bill and JoAn retired in February 1988 after 33 years in the business. A couple of months later, Zach's chicken was declared the best in town via a *Journal-Review* survey. Reid Duffy of "Duffy's Diner" featured Bill, Jim, and his wife Karen in a short segment. Jim purchased the business at his parents' retirement and another generation of Zach's all worked. Their son Jay was manager, Suzie waitress, and Karen call-in help. Jim ran the business until a great influx of franchised restaurants took over the south end of town. On Christmas Eve, 1996, the Zachs said final good-byes to many customers and employees who had also become good friends. The Wray family had a wonderful establishment atop a hill and down the highway from Zach's. Their Redwood Inn's sugar cream pie was to die for. Uncle Smiley's on Waynetown Road is one of the few older down-home places left.

One of the most popular questions a Montgomery County historian gets is, "What is the Supreme Tribe of Ben Hur?" To answer that easily, it is a fraternal insurance society. It was created by David W. Gerard. David was born on July 7, 1844 in Shelby County, Ohio. In 1849, his family moved to Romney, Indiana where his father Abner owned a general store. Shortly after arriving in Indiana, however, Abner died. The Gerards had three boys, and the young widow also had six other children by a former marriage. She packed up the family and returned on a canal boat to Sidney, Ohio. According to an article of John Bowerman's, Lew Wallace, an inspiring young lawyer at the time, settled Abner's small estate. David received a good education back in Ohio and became a teacher at 16, but his patriotism called him to enlist in the 8th Ohio Battery. After the war, David, his mother, and brothers came back to Indiana, this time to Montgomery County where he taught at Pleasant Hill (Wingate). He met and married his wife, Elizabeth Krug, a member of a prominent Coal Creek Township family. They moved to Crawfordsville where he became active in insurance and real estate. He and Frank Snyder, along with former Crawfordsville mayor Samuel Voris, founded the Indiana and Ohio Live Stock Insurance Company, which soon became one of Indiana's top insurance companies.

Gerard and Lew Wallace formed a binding friendship about this time. Wallace had completed his famous novel and Gerard perused it carefully. Bowerman said, "Our subject was evidently greatly inspired by the picture Wallace painted of the lowly Nazarene who went about doing good." At any rate, Gerard's germ of a benevolent society took place about this time and, in 1893, Gerard, Snyder, Voris, and Dr. J.F. Davidson decided the following:

> The time was ripe for launching the dream that had continued to grow in the mind of Gerard. He had been so impressed with the novel of his friend and neighbor Lew Wallace, that he felt it could be the basis for a ritual to be used in the society. Wallace was consulted and promptly gave his consent to use the name Ben Hur, but suggested that it be

The Ben Hur Life Association building is located on Main Street. The 1941 building has been a symbol to Crawfordsville for more than 60 years, but at the time of publication, its fate is unknown.

> called Tribe of Ben Hur rather than the original thought of Knights of Ben Hur.

The ideas of the society were to promote truth, benevolence, honor, love, righteousness, loyalty, and peace. Harper and Brothers, publishers of the novel, gave consent to use the name and, on January 9, 1894, the articles of incorporation of the Supreme Tribe of Ben Hur were filed with the state of Indiana. On March 1, a large number of guests gathered at Crawfordsville for the installation of officers. Although former Indiana governor Ira J. Chase was the first supreme chief, Gerard himself held the office for several years prior to his death. By April 1896, courts had been created in a dozen states. In 1909, their assets totaled 1.5 million. In 1930, the name Ben Hur Life Association was adopted. By 1933, assets for the association totaled $10 million. Insurance claim checks usually went out in the return mail. The Ben Hur Home for the aged and dependent members was owned by the association. In 1940, "30 inmates were in the home. That same year, the Association employed almost 600 people; 70 in Crawfordsville alone."

The cornerstone of the Ben Hur Building was laid a year and three months after the death of Gerard. Fittingly, David W. Gerard's son Royal presided at the ceremony. Royal's son Dave was one of Crawfordsville's best-loved mayors. One of Crawfordsville's most beautiful buildings is still the Ben Hur.

Many people will remember the grand hotel in downtown Crawfordsville on the corner of Main and Green. The Crawford Hotel opened its doors on February

22, 1900. Much of the furniture came from the Ramsey Hotel. The Crawford had its own water and electric supplies. The dining room was on the second floor with a mosaic floor. Bedrooms totaled almost 100, many with their own bathroom. An elaborate oak stairway lead to the upper floors. Portable fire escapes in the middle of the building dropped chains so that a fire didn't seem to be such a threat. Various businesses were on the bottom floor of the Crawford, including a café, barbershop, security and loan business, drugstore, clothing store, the Crawford Bar, a telegraph office, and a tailor shop to name a few.

An opening banquet of the Crawford took place on March 7, 1900. The next day's *Journal* noted that there "were men present from all the businesses and professions in the city and they made a good looking crowd." The menu consisted of several unusual dishes: Lynn Haven Bays, Sauterne, Olives, Consomme Royal, Black Bass Stuffed, Crayfish Sauce, Pommes Parisienne, Claret, Frog Hams, En Crumbs, Early June Peas, Roman Punch, Jack Snipe stuffed and roasted, Mayonnaise of Fresh Shrimps, Cabernet, Ice Cream with Strawberries, Assorted Cake, Coffee, and Cigars. There were 120 guests. An article by Marsh Jones (February 1984) reported, "Speakers and their topics were: H.H. Ristine, Crawford and the Crawford, M.W. Bruner, Crawfordsville Men Old and New, A.D. Thomas, Crawfordsville Women, and W.T. Whittington, Crawfordsville Council." Lew Wallace was scheduled to speak, but was sick that evening. As Jones pointed out, "there was regular service on the railroads and the interurban

The Crawford Hotel, in existence from 1900 to 1974, was run by the Jones family for the majority of these years.

at this time. Salesmen would come to town and spend several days selling wares. Catalogs did not exist."

Now, here's why Marsh Jones wrote the article on the Crawford: the hotel was managed by several generations of the Jones family. Marsh's great-grandfather W.D. Jones died in 1903, "so he was not long engaged in active management of the hotel." W.D.'s son Ammon "Am" Jones ran the hotel until 1922. Marshal H. Jones Sr. took over until the hotel was sold in 1948. Marsh said that the biggest problem facing the hotel was the Great Depression, as salesmen often left IOUs versus real cash. In the 1940s, Marsh said a single room without a bath cost $1.25. "A double was $5.50, the better rooms being magnificent, spacious and containing large bay windows." The hotel stood on the northeast corner of Green and Main. Marsh himself was an active member of the Crawfordsville community, having served 30 years on the Montgomery County Council, as did his father did. Marsh learned international morse code during World War II and this led to his lifetime love of ham radio.

About the time of the Crawford opening, a major price war was going on between the two big downtown department stores—Grahams (located where Schloots is today) and Warner/Peck's. A Graham's ad in early 1901 was quite impressive and was tagged as a "Department Manager's Sale." Each manager's picture and prices were on the full-page ad. Dora Hardee, white goods department, said she had the lowest prices ever known with bedspreads (68 by 80 inches) for 35¢. Hugh Kelsey's picture loomed especially large as Graham's carpet manager since he had worked at a competitor's, Louis Bischof's, which was a huge establishment.

Sol and Max Tannenbaum also had the "first clothing house in Crawfordsville, their rooms elegantly fitted and handsomely furnished with a novel stock of the latest styles in the market." Yet, it was Grahams and Warner/Peck's who were constantly warring.

Martin's Ice Company burned to the ground in 1890, but the company continued under the guidance of its creator, William Martin, and his son William K. It was William who started the first dairy business in the city in 1873, which naturally led to the ice industry. His son graduated from Crawfordsville High School and Wabash College. William K. was a man about town, also serving as a director of the Citizens National Bank, manager of the Crawfordsville Heating Company, a trustee of the Electric Company, and holding interest in the Home Telephone Company.

Orpheus Milton Gregg headed the Match Factory for many years, but delved into other businesses as well. He was born on October 7, 1848, the son of Samuel, who was the son of Alpheus, an early pioneer. Samuel had a large hardware store in Crawfordsville. Orpheus managed the Indiana Wire Company, was president of the Columbia Wire and Fence Company, was on the board of the Dovetail Buggy Company, a promoter of the local Box Company, a director of Elston Bank, and organized the Gregg, Coutant, and Gregg Mitten and Glove Company. Sons Frederick, Charles, and Caleb were also active businessmen in Crawfordsville. The Bosse Glove Factory (previously named Gregg's) was located on East Pike. It was in existence not long after the turn of the century and was here up until about 1930. It was a hot, lint-filled place, but one where women could find reasonably-paid work.

Likely, one of our most unique and longest standing businesses was the Crawfordsville Casket Plant, which stemmed from a small cabinet shop. William Robertson went into business building his factory on the corner of Pike and Washington Streets. At that time, the area was a forest. This and other virgin timbers of the area made many of the first caskets. In 1868, the company began making coffins and became the Crawfordsville Coffin Company. About this time, the company built a nice building at 309 West Pike. The February 26, 1874 *Crawfordsville Journal* stated that the company had, "a large assortment of metallic and wood coffins and caskets, along with robes and shrouds." Robertson remained with the company for over 50 years. He was a strict business manager, yet was known as "a fair and kindly, plain Scot noted for his sterling honesty," as stated in his obituary. At the time of Robertson's death, his partner was Robert E. Bryant, a Wabash College graduate. Bryant had been a prisoner during the Civil War, having served under Lew Wallace. He was the first telegraph operator in the city. Another partner, Paul Houston Burns, was also a veteran.

In 1891, 53 workers were employed making coffins and there were twice that many employees at the turn of the century. In 1903, Claude Ewoldt took over as the head of the company's operations and remained as such for close to 50 years. Sol Tannenbaum became an officer in the company, along with C.M. Crawford, M.B. and Joseph Binford, Henry Campbell, M.F. Manson, and C.O. McFarland. In 1923, caskets ranged from a pine, double-lid box for $10 to a bronze-handled, silk-lined Cadillac for over $200. The price doubled 20 years later. In 1929, the Casket Company was touted as the oldest industry in Crawfordsville at that time. In 1946, the company added the manufacturing of radio cabinets. These were veneered and made from the finest gum and poplar woods, finished in dark mahogany. Motorola received 5,000 mahogany cabinets with FM/AM short wave connections. A Quonset structure of 100 feet by 40 feet was built west of the old 120-foot by 30-foot casket manufacturing center. The rough lumber had to be air-dried for six months before use, then put in a dry kiln before being made into the finished product. The Casket Company sponsored a local basketball team for several years and closed its doors about 1960.

Located in a farming community, it is proper to mention Crabbs, Reynolds, and Taylor, a seed cleaning, feed manufacturing company that also operated several elevators in Central Indiana. In 1929, there were almost 80 employees. Crabbs's daughter Mary Virginia Shaw will be remembered by most readers of this work as the quaint old lady who lived across from Lane Place and always wore a crazy hat. Busenbark Grain Company operated eight elevators and was Crabbs's main competition in the city. Other early established businesses were Birch & Birch, which repaired machines for area factories; Johnson Manufacturing, which manufactured lighting systems; Puritan Water Softeners; Crawfordsville Shake Brick Company, which employed over 50 and had 11 kilns; W.Q. O'Neall, the birthplace of corrugated iron culverts; and Umphreys, manufacturers of library tables and other furniture.

The Wilson Brothers Shirt Factory was another long-term business, employing hundreds from the local workforce. Four brothers (John, E. Crane, Hugh, and Milton) owned a retail clothing store in Cincinnati and later moved to Chicago. In 1893, the brothers took up a whole Chicago block. Wilson Brothers expansion to Crawfordsville came in 1937 when they built a 40-by-40-foot (with a 40-by-40-foot wing) steel and brick building at 1000 Lane Avenue (where the Lane Nursing Home is today). General Manager Walter Stegman said that our fair city was centrally located, and modern and progressive in its business and public affairs. He discussed Crawfordsville as a typical model city that should prove a splendid home for any industry. In the 1947 *Journal-Review* business series, an article stated that there were 90 employees at the Crawfordsville plant with an annual payroll of $150,000.

From Cincinnati to Chicago, South Bend to Crawfordsville, the company acquired other branches in Indiana, as well as Wisconsin, New York, and New Hampshire. John Kimbrell was plant manager in 1947. Colorful sports shirts in lightweight cotton were the specialty in Crawfordsville's plant. The cloth was spread out on a 180-foot table, 240 ply high. The laying of the pattern and cutting with an electric knife took highly skilled employees. Collars, pockets, and sleeves were trimmed by hand and sent as bundles to the sewing area. An assembly system existed, passing the materials from one operation to the next. Visitors to the plant

The Crawfordsville Casket Company's basketball team takes a grim view of the sport. Team members include, from left to right, (front row) Chuck Henry, Earl Peck, Robert Sparger, Greg Layne, and Alva Brannon; (back row) Ed Servies, Harry Haybarger, Darrel Warbitton, and Don Haffner.

Wilson Brothers Shirt Factory, with a plant on Lane Avenue from 1937 to 1958, was a large Crawfordsville employer for over 20 years.

especially enjoyed the buttonhole machines. After each shirt was completed, it was inspected and boxed for shipping. The not-so-perfect shirts called "seconds" could be purchased by the employees. Crawfordsville employees mostly agreed that it was one of the best places to work. One said, "The place was clean and the people were lovely." But all good things come to an end, so on January 23, 1958, Wilson Brothers sold the building and moved the factory to Kentucky. Many still remember Wilson Brothers shirts were "garments for the well-dressed American male!"

Speaking of men's clothing, Stecks, a store owned by Herschel Steck, originated in Muncie. Harold Nixon (Nick) began working for Steck while he was in junior high school, through high school, and later on in college. After his graduation, he formed a partnership with Steck and opened the Crawfordsville store, which celebrated its 50th anniversary in 1986. By 1964, Nick owned all of the store and considered changing the name, yet Nick felt "Stecks stood for quality and service." About this time, the Weathervane, a lady's apparel store, was opened. A store in Lafayette was also opened. Nick had financed his own way from his early years. One nearly half-century employee, Maurice Oakley, stated that Nick was most kind and considerate of everyone. He loved God, family, friends, and his store. He married Crawfordsville High School (and Indiana University) graduate Jane Dunnington and they had two children, Wade and Kim.

His beloved wife passed away in 1970, then Nick married childhood acquaintance Mary Ellen Hathaway. She made sure Nick was comfortable during his final days. After Nick's death, his children continued to own the Crawfordsville store, but closed the Lafayette one. Sandy (Arthur) and wife Rita Harpel (who had worked for Nick in the Weathervane in Lafayette), came to Crawfordsville at this time to run the business for Nick's children. They closed the store in early 1991. Later that year, the Harpels began a new adventure (in the same building) by opening a unique and enjoyable small eatery appropriately called "Arthur's." Becky Hurt, an employee of the Nixon's, branched off to start her own business (The Homestead, at 111 North Washington), similar to the one she ran for them (The Attic), which is currently one of the best shops in town. Today, men purchase fine menswear at Mac's.

A factory with an interesting background is Hoosier-Crown (H-C). Robert B. "Bob" Smith began with $160 cash and an idea. He improvised an experimental lab in a small room on Pine Street. When Smith realized his idea had some worth and his little makeshift plant was insufficient, he moved his operation to North Walnut Street where McDaniel Freight was in the 1940s. He hired about a dozen workers. In 1947, his expanded business was featured in the Crawfordsville paper in their "Know Your Industrial Crawfordsville" series. That year, Hoosier-Crown employed 80 people and had about 20 modern machines, occupying 50,000 square feet and manufacturing about 400 million bottle caps per year. Automatic equipment at the time could produce 1,800 bottle caps per minute. Smith wasn't satisfied. His personal goal was to gross $10 million that year. Steel for the plant came in large sheets, each sheet producing about 352 caps. Dr. Pepper, Royal Crown Cola, 7-Up, and Cliquot were some of the companies Hoosier-Crown supplied with bottle caps.

In the 1947 article, Smith showed concern that the steel and cork was not up to prewar excellence. He used his creativity again during the war years, recycling easily available tin cans for the caps and used paper for the corks. In 1986, H-C was purchased by the Aluminum Company of America. In 1990, the Lafayette Business Digest reported H-C was 59,000 square feet of buildings at 1201 East Elmore, employing 300 with an international business. Pepsi, Coke, Shell, and Penzoil were major customers. Today, the company is known as Crown Cork and Seal, employs over 100, and is located on Walnut Street.

Healthcare is important to us all and four generations of Esther Houston's family have been in the healthcare business. In 1970, Esther took over the Ben Hur Nursing Home from her mother Martha Williams, who originally began the facility with 62 beds, according to a May 1993 *Montgomery County Magazine* article written by Glen Cumbarelis. Esther Houston's grandmother in turn had a real "nursing home," as she cared for people in her private house. Esther's sons are also part of the Ben Hur Nursing Home and Williamsburg Health Care Facility. Mrs. Houston said in the article that, although there are mounds of paperwork, the rewards are worth it: "I love working with the residents and I've enjoyed the employees." In fact, the above article concluded, "I've had lots of good help over the years!" The Lane House and Carmen are excellent nursing homes as well. Today, a fairly new concept is to live in an assisted-care facility when aged.

Crawfordsville wouldn't be Crawfordsville without a publishing company for our most literary city. The big one that comes to mind is of course R.R. Donnelley & Son (RRD). Richard Robert Donnelley started his publishing business in Chicago in 1864. By 1906, his son Thomas desired to expand the business. He wanted a small town atmosphere. *The Quilt Chronicles* tell us, "Skilled investigators surveyed every town within a 200-mile radius. Crawfordsville was chosen for its size, its beautiful shaded streets, nice homes, and a fine spirit of Americanism. It also was the seat of Wabash College and had a remarkable high school building occupying a whole square."

It was not until 1921 when the first Crawfordsville Donnelley Plant was established, however. This was in a defunct Absorber Company. High school boys were trained in typesetting by a craftsman sent out from the Chicago plant. By the fall of 1921, the presses were rolling, with 24 employees, 6 of whom were women. Two of the first hired were James Footit and George Manson. The first apprentice graduation was in 1928 with Thomas E. Donnelley himself giving a talk titled, "Our Vision of a Country Press." Lenley Mill was the first of the "original" apprentices. In less than two years, it was clear that a larger space was needed; thus, the Sloan Street Plant was built. Within a few short years, the original 33 acres purchased on Sloan Street had expanded to 84,000 square feet.

Donnelley has sponsored many teams in the area, including girls' basketball as early as the 1930s. Sam Hart was put in charge (along with George Collar) of the offset department in November 1933. He thought the bosses crazy, as George didn't even know what offset printing was, but of course he learned. Buck Jones came from a farm making $1.25 a week, so he was thrilled with bringing home $12 a week in 1937 working at Donnelley. From the original 24 employees, by the end of 1930, there were almost 500. In 1941, a new wing was added to the Sloan Street plant and the well-known tower was added. Alma McCarty noted the loss of men in the war years by saying, "With all the men in the service, it meant I became a supervisor." When Alma retired in 1970, she had worked at RRD for almost 45 years. Many employees have logged decades in what most consider "the best 'lil factory in town." Robert Bratton, a graduate apprentice worker, was the city's first Gold Star, having been killed in World War II in September 1943.

As RRD finished out the 1940s, they won awards for production and perfection. Through the 1950s, production tripled. The majority of what is printed in Crawfordsville includes encyclopedias, Reader's Digest Condensed Books, Time, Inc. publications, and bibles. The South Donnelley plant was built in 1964, with the explicit task to print the *World Book Encyclopedia*. Over 80 years after its beginning, Crawfordsville Donnelley's employs 1,800 and has almost 2 million square feet in its various facilities, most of which are still at the Sloan Street plant and the Highway 32 West plant.

R.R. Donnelley and Sons Publishing Company has employed a multitude for over 80 years in Crawfordsville. This is an early view of the plant.

We couldn't speak of the furniture business without mentioning one of our well-known stores. Garrett Schloot moved to Crawfordsville and opened Schloot Furniture in 1933 in a corner of the Ben Hur Building. The same month that Schloots opened on Main Street, Minnie Petts Flower Shop opened there, and another furniture store opened (Coulter-Smock). Schloot's advertising has always been unique and began with "The Key to Economy," the key symbolizing opportunity for great values and low prices. Shortly after opening, Schloot offered a new Philco radio "which would not only get the regular stations, but also airplane communications and ALL police calls." The radio sold for just $37.50, but was on sale for only $30.

Expansion forced a move in 1939 to the present location, 117 North Washington Street. In 1937, Bob Schloot joined his father in the business. Garrett's other son Loren joined the business upon his return from the service. The three ran the store for quite a few years. In 1952, the old metal storefront was replaced with a new glass one. Bob's son Tom worked in the business as a teenager during his college days, and today runs the store. Tom is married to a wonderful, civic-minded lady, Patty, and they are the parents of two daughters, Amy and Martha. When Tom's father would go to North Carolina to buy furniture, he would tell everyone about his great little city, how it was economically, industrially, and agriculturally strong. Well, the Schloot family is proud of their little town and Crawfordsville is proud to have such a fine furniture store. Carrico and R-B were here for quite some time, too.

One of the most unusual buildings downtown today is located on North Green Street and was built in 1854 by a local doctor, Simon Bennage. From a *Review* article, "the new two-story brick building would replace the log structures formerly owned by Ephraim Griffith, Harmon Stultz, and John Brady. It is speculated that one of those log buildings may have been the original Ristine Tavern." The editor of the *Review* was quite impressed with this new building, as he had often commented that downtown Crawfordsville was "shoddy" with its crude huts. Editor Brown must have been an influence, as not long afterward, downtown Crawfordsville began perhaps its first revitalization. Dr. Bennage did not use his new building for his medical practice, but instead rented it out. A Terre Hautian, J.L. Brown opened a new clothing store there. This didn't last long. The building became a grocery thereafter. W.B. Keeney had a tobacco barn there as well. Other businesses in the building included a farmer's market, a drugstore, and a blacksmith.

Enter Otto Schlemmer, a German-born immigrant. It was Schlemmer who did much of the restructuring to the beautiful building. He was a saloon keeper and had a large family, some of whom became quite important to Crawfordsville's history. His son George took over the saloon and was well-respected in the community. Another son, Fritz, was one of Crawfordsville's most talented artists. Otto's daughter Hildegarde was a Methodist missionary in India and Emily, another daughter, was an exceptional pianist. The Schlemmer heirs sold the building to Bill Endicott and a variety of small businesses were there, including restaurants, shoe repair, billiards, an engineering firm, and a license branch. Red Cab was also there for a while. Thankfully, the law firm of Berry and Tully restored the building to the beauty it is today.

The inside of Collin's Barber Shop, from left to right, shows Jesse Collins, Floyd Suiters, unknown, Evan Bannon, and Bill Moore.

Bill Carpenter has been cutting hair for more than 45 years as of September 2002. He took a nine-month course at International Barber College, then served a one-year internship with "Slim" Greves of Darlington. At this time, haircuts were $1 ($8 today). Bill said he made $35 his first week, all in cash; 30 percent went to Greves for chair rental. When Carpenter moved to Crawfordsville, one of his goals was to make the same amount of money as a Donnelley worker, but Bill doesn't know if he ever accomplished that goal. His first little building was where Brown's Car Sales is today, later moving to his famous little red barn on the old Pizza Hut site. When the new Pizza Hut was built behind this building, Bill moved his little place to the South Boulevard site of today. He's had some good times, one of them being the fact that he has cut four generations of hair. The Lewis Newkirk family (son Dave, grandson Joe, and great-grandson Cody) was the first four-generation group. Bill said his most interesting haircut was not long ago when he cut a set of dreadlocks. "I've never put a comb in anything like that in my life. The guy probably had tears in his eyes when I got done, but I got 'em all!" One thing he's never done was cut a woman's hair. Keith Parker was with Carpenter for awhile and they still get together once a month to cut each other's hair, but Bill says (with a smile) that Keith has the most to cut. Some great barbershops have been around, such as the Crawford Barber Shop, Hutson's, Jim's, Collins, and Plaza, but one of the longer-standing barbering establishments is Englewood, dating back to the 1960s. However, hair styling is quickly snuffing out this profession. Currently, there are over two dozen places to get your hair "styled."

Probably the first exclusive shoe store in the city was the Youngman Company, owned by William Youngman and his son Robert. Two Montgomery County brothers purchased it in 1919 and ran Burroughs Brothers Shoes for many years. Kenney's Shoes was downtown for decades and many shoes were purchased in Goodman's basement as well.

Throughout the years, larger car dealers have been Crawfordsville Ford, Perry Lewis Ford, Crawfordsville Nash Sales, Oliver K. Galloway, Gould's, Clements, Horners, Montgomery Motor Company, Larry Cummings, Town Edge Motors, and Herman Davis. In the early days of the automobile, gasoline sales were mostly capped by George W. Deere (supplying Red Hat Gas to over 40 stations in the 1920s and 1930s). "Brothers" Lawrence and Sam Boots began Boots Brothers Oil Company over 50 years ago. Today, Phil and Fafy Boots own and operate the business. Wrecker services having been around for quite some time are Froedge's and Wilson's.

The undertaking business has been around for a very long time and so has the Hunt family. Walter Lawrence Hunt received his education in Montgomery County schools. He graduated from Askins' College of Embalming in Indianapolis in 1912. In 1916, he started a funeral home in Crawfordsville. Twenty-one years later, he went into business with Noble Reeves under the name Hunt and Reeves Morticians. Noble had early Montgomery County roots. He was a CHS graduate and, like Hunt, an Askins graduate. Reeves was involved with the Masons, Eastern Star, Rotary, American Legion, and other organizations. Hunt married

Georgiane Bowman and had five children, son Robert going into business with his father. Tom Hunt, Robert's son, joined his father upon graduation from embalming school. Today, Rob and David Hunt help their father Tom carry on the family legacy.

William Lawrence Murphy was the grandson of two sets of Irish immigrants and operated the Utterback & Murphy Funeral Home at 300 South Grant with partner John Utterback. Other longtime funeral homes include Brights, Burkharts, and Powers & Priebe. Tombstones go along with this topic and Crawfordsville Monument (by various names) has been at 116 West Market for many decades.

Along that same line, several doctors were either born, bred, or stayed in our area for many years. Just a few are Keith Baird, Thomas Cooksey, Robert Cornell, Fred Daugherty, Richard Eggers, Thomas Haller, Marion Kirtley, Sam Millis, Jose Peralta, Wesley Shannon, and Vic Viray. Dentists include John Beeson, John Bushong, Fred Cantrell, R.E. Halle, William Peacock, John Turchi, Winston Warren, and John Walker. Cash Furr and Harold Lambert were two of the first chiropractors. Mary Callahan, Phil Grush, Cloyd Haffner, Carl Shroeder, and Caster Wilson were optometrists. On the professional line, Ault, Beemer, Bounnell, Groves, Harding, Harris, Husted, McGaughey, Milligan, Wernle, and Young are just a few of the long-standing lawyers. Sommer was our highly-respected county judge for many years. Thanks to the Polk Directories, it is an easy task to overview the folks of Crawfordsville, whether they be insurance agents, grocers, photographers, butchers, bakers, or candlestick makers!

Manufacturing is varied in the city today. Just south of Crawfordsville (Whitesville) is one of our largest employers. Two railroads, easy truck access, an electric substation, and flat land lured the Nucor Steel Company to our area in the late 1980s. Today, it employs 600 local folks. The Raybestos-Manhatten Company, Wabash Division came to town in 1951, the cost of the plant having been built at about $1 million. LeRoy Musselman was appointed plant manager. The plant began with about 100 employees, making transmission parts for tanks during the Korean War. A celebration of 50 years was held recently. Today, Raybestos employs over 700 and has an international market in clutch and brake friction products.

Located at 1615 East Elmore, Lithonia Lighting has been here for over 30 years, manufacturing and distributing a wide variety of lighting fixtures for commercial, industrial, and residential buildings. Norcote was established the same year as Lithonia and supplies Donnelley's and others with screen printing inks, labels, and other printing supplies. In 2002, Pace Dairy completed its 20th year in Crawfordsville. The packaging of cheese by over 200 employees is the main thrust of the company. California Pellet Mill's Crawfordsville Division at 1114 East Wabash began in 1946. About 100 workers make dyes and roller shelves for pellet machines used in making animal feed, fertilizer, and other products. Crawford Industries, located at 1414 Crawford Drive, was established here in 1959. Fleetwood Travel Trailers is located at 1635 Elmore Street. It opened its Crawfordsville doors in 1971. A couple of the smaller present industries in the city include Terra Products (pumps and valves) and W&M Plastics (plastic injection moldings).

At this writing, B&D Lumber, a local legend for about 50 years, is closing its doors. Pools (owned by Representative Dan Pool) became Stevenson's Ace Hardware. Dillmans and Galeys Hardwares were in existence for several years. Luckily, the Whitecotton family's Town and Country and Thrifty Supply are still going strong. Of course, some of the items can also be purchased at Target and Wal-Mart.

Bed and breakfasts have become popular in recent years. The Holiday Inn has been joined by several motels near the interstate. The Riviera on the southside of town near the newly-redone mall is still owned and managed by Norma Miller whose parents began the motel many years ago.

Many businesses have come and gone and this chapter represents only a small percentage of the many people and their places in our Athens city.

This memorial honors one of Crawfordsville's most respected citizens, Howard Sommer, who served as a judge here for many years and was extensively involved in the community.

7. Clubs and Organizations

As with the business chapter, the clubs and organizations could go on and on. We'll discuss some of the more unique clubs and others that are longstanding, but not every club to exist in our fair city. Fittingly, we begin this chapter with a brief history of the historical society. The group's birth was in 1911. The public library housed many exhibits in the society's early years. Twenty years later, Lane Place became the permanent home of the Montgomery County Historical Society. From 30 members that year to over 600 today, the society publishes a variety of history books, hosts historical and educational trips, maintains the original beauty of the Henry S. Lane Home, and sponsors the Strawberry Festival and Christmas tours yearly. Another anticipated yearly event is the annual Tannenbaum Dinner where local grade schoolers read historical essays. The event honors Max Tannenbaum, local businessman, who donated much time and funds to the group. Tours are given to hundreds of visitors from around the world. In 2002, John Hardwick served as president of the board, following Don Fine, who will resume leadership in 2003.

Probably the oldest of the local organizations is the Masons. Isaac C. Elston and five others began work on the charter as early as April 1843. The Montgomery Lodge No. 50 charter was granted on May 27, 1844. On the 60th anniversary, the present lodge that even non-Masonic members know and love was dedicated. Five Masonic bodies merged together in the 1890s with the dream of building a remarkable lodge building. Businessmen A.F. Ramsey, Walter Hulet, George Graham, Albert Miller, and Charles Goltra comprised the building committee. William Sharpe, a Lodge No. 50 member, served as architect, while members Ben Myers and Nathaniel Swan did the brickwork with the first brick being laid September 3, 1901. On October 3, a more formal dedication took place with Thomas R. Marshall, Wabash College graduate (later two-term governor of Indiana and vice president of the United States), as speaker. Harvey Hazelrigg was the first worshipful master.

Upon the formal building dedication on May 27, 1904, George Grimes (Ladoga), grand master of Indiana, was in charge of that service. Lew Wallace spoke at this event. In 1912, a pipe organ was installed. In 1915, a kitchen expansion took place. Major Lucien Foote served as secretary for 42 years and worshipful master in 1874.

Lane Place, home of Henry S. Lane, is owned and maintained by the Montgomery County Historical Society.

Jere West, Montgomery Circuit Court judge for 32 years, served as Lodge No. 50 master and both men served as Indiana's grand master. A deputy grand master was one of Montgomery County's famous Civil War generals, Mahlon Manson. The original cost of the building and its furnishing was $46,000 with the complete cost being paid off within four years. A recent renovation to the inside took place and everyone involved got a big scare as part of the side of the building began caving in while digging for a new city building. All is well now and the Masonic Temple still remains one of Crawfordsville's most beautiful buildings. Eliza Moffett, wife of Dr. Thomas Moffett, was the first matron of the Athens Chapter, Eastern Star. The Order of the Eastern Star meets there, as well as other organizations.

The Daughters of the American Revolution received its charter on June 13, 1898. There were 14 charter members, the name Dorothy Q (from a poem by Oliver Wendell Holmes) having been suggested by member Sophia Crane Ristine. Josephine Tuttle Thomas was elected the first regent. She was the wife of Charles Lambert Thomas, a Civil War veteran and prominent lawyer. Josephine's sisters Katharine and Susan were charter members as well. Alice Green Ross was Dorothy Q's only state regent, but many of the past and present members have served as various state officials. In 1902, a bronze tablet was purchased by Joseph Tuttle, president of Wabash College and father of Josephine, with the names of Revolutionary soldiers who were buried in Montgomery County. The tablet was in the Wabash College Library for many years, was later moved to the post office, and is now on the front of the DAR

The Dorothy Q Daughters of the American Revolution House, located at 400 East Wabash, was the home of Isaac C. Elston Jr.

house at 400 East Wabash. Several DAR markers have been placed throughout the county, not only on Revolutionary soldier's graves, but also on the grave of Lewis and Clark Expedition member William Bratton, who in 2002 received an Indiana historical marker dedicated by the Waynetown community and the Ohio River Chapter of the Lewis and Clark Trail Heritage Foundation, a plate on a room at the old Culver Hospital (the chapter had furnished the room), and a bronze tablet at the Lew Wallace Study.

The DAR has sponsored a local Children of the American Revolution Chapter in two timeframes. The first group was named the Isham Floyd and the second the Susan E. Wallace Society (after Lew Wallace's wife, Susan Elston). The first was established in 1924, but it is not known how long this group lasted. The second, an extremely active group for several years, began in 1969. Four state CAR presidents were from this later group: Mike Howell, Jeff Bennett, Jay Zach, and Rich Otten. Sadly, in 2003, there is no CAR in Crawfordsville.

The Good Citizen Award was started in 1936 with 10 girls from the 10 county high schools participating. Florence Oltman from Crawfordsville won the state contest in 1939. A major community project done by the chapter was the nine-volume cemetery inscriptions (Donnis Widener's regent's project), of which copies are used daily at the Crawfordsville District Public Library. Also, Bible records were collected for many years.

In 1926, Dorothy Q purchased the Isaac C. Elston Jr. home. Colonel Elston had built the house in 1882 in a beautiful Queen Anne style. It was his son Isaac

Elston III who offered the home to the DAR. The Elston Memorial House Board was incorporated in 1928. Present board chair is Lela Lofland and her sister-in-law Sandy is regent. A large open house celebration for DQ's 100th birthday was held with several state officials visiting and outgoing regent Nancy Pickel in charge. Few people in Crawfordsville do not recognize the DAR house, which was red with green trim for many years, but was recently painted white with gray edging.

There were a total of 15 in the Kulinary Kraft Klub in 1910. At monthly meetings, the gals put on frills and the best spread of goodies in town. Although many were married, men were never allowed at the affairs. When Myrtle Beatrice Schenck Nader's husband died and she moved in with her brother Dr. Schenck, the club relaxed the "no men" rule and let the doctor eat with them. Later, husbands and children were added. The club remained intact until the gals got older and began to pass away.

As strong today as in its beginning years, the Sunshine Society of Crawfordsville High School is over 100 years old as well. Much of the Sunshine Society's work is done at Christmastime. In 1905, 60 baskets were delivered to deprived families. In the 1950s, the girls sold saltwater taffy with proceeds going to Riley Hospital. No one can put a number on those individuals who have been touched by the Sunshine girls, but it is safe to say that thousands have been given good cheer.

In 1900, the Crawfordsville High School Gamma Delta, fondly referred to as the Owl's Club, began. Carrie and Mary Hannah Krout were founding members, along with Jo Graham (her husband being James E. Evans, a longtime First National Bank cashier), Laura Williams (wife of Benjamin Franklin Crabbs, local businessman), Emma Ashenhurt (wife of William Sidener), Meg Purviance (daughter of Dr. Samuel and wife of attorney Melvin Bruner), Mellie Blair (a teacher in Crawfordsville for 42 years), and Mattie Keeney (daughter of Jere Keeney, newspaper editor), who was a court reporter for several years. These eight women were very close in life and in death, buried near each other in Oak Hill Cemetery.

Crawfordsville began its Girl Scout troop under the guidance of Ursula Ward, according to an article by Jean White. In the summer of 1925, several troops camped in tents along Sugar Creek near the Yount Hotel. The dining hall of the hotel was used for eats and a large area in the lobby was used for craft activities. Frank Evans, who lived nearby, supplied freshwater and showed picture shows to the girls. Swans, peacocks, and deer roamed around his house, which helped to entertain the girls. Civil War veteran Captain H.H. Talbot visited one evening to tell the girls how to make useful items for camping. In the spring of 1929, a specific local goal was reached by our Girl Scouts by selling cookies baked by a local store, Eckers. Garden seeds were also sold. A drinking fountain for Culver Hospital was bought and dedicated by the girls. Marie Glover became Montgomery County's first to receive the Girl Scout's highest honor, the Golden Eaglet, in 1933. A favorite Girl Scout Christmastime affair was to carol door to door.

By the end of the 1930s, about 50 girls were in three troops in all of Montgomery County. In the 1940s, the number grew to over 500 girls with 65 leaders. Daughter and father banquets have been popular throughout the years as well. By June 1941, the Girl Scouts added a Brownie Troop. Mrs. Carol Klinger was the organizer. In April 1942, the Girl Scout Association of Montgomery County was chartered. In 1957, Montgomery joined Tippecanoe, under the Tippecanoe Girl Scout Council. The name changed to Sycamore Girl Scout Council, Inc. in 1968. Seven other counties were added at this time. Daisys were added in 1985. This level is for kindergarten-age girls. Girls today go to Camp Talitha located near Deers' Mill in Southern Montgomery County. In 2002, the Girl Scouts organization was 90 years old.

The Flower Lover's Club was organized in 1921 as the "Dahlia Club." The club has held many annual flower shows and has been responsible for much sprucing up of the city.

The Crawfordsville Kiwanis Club was organized around Christmas, 1921. It was extremely active in the 1940s to 1960s and has had many important men in its head position, including Richard Ristine (local man who became lieutenant governor of the state) and Dr. Ted Gronert (Wabash professor and historical writer).

Bob Wernle, longtime lawyer, headed the Ouiatenon Club in 1957. Their group was founded in November 1883 for the specific purpose of "literary, scientific and culture."

Delta Theta Tau (Epsilon Omega chapter) was organized in Crawfordsville on September 6, 1934, but went inactive during the war years. In April 1948, the chapter reorganized and has remained one of Crawfordsville's most philanthropic groups. It will be remembered especially for its Tour of Homes and strawberry ice cream booth at the Strawberry Festival. Gloria Long is current president.

In the late 1940s, there were 54 Home Demonstration clubs in the county. The Boy's Club began about this time as well. Another local group, the Optimist Club, sold Christmas trees for many years to help support the Boy's Club. Recently, a new Boy's and Girl's Club (largely supported by the Morrison family) was built at 1001 Whitlock Avenue.

The Lion's Club was organized in 1932, the first club president being Forrest Howell. He was the longtime owner of Indiana Printing, followed by his son Dick.

Our local Red Cross turned 85 in 2002. Dr. N. Austin Carey urged area citizens to form a Red Cross for needed war supplies. About 100 women gathered for a meeting to plan the local chapter—the local name being suggested as the Lew Wallace Chapter. Within a week after petitioning the War Department, the local group was approved for organization, but the chapter name was nixed and replaced with the required geographical name of Montgomery County Chapter, American Red Cross. The first official meeting took place at the high school on March 2, 1917. Dr. Carey told the group what was needed for a successful chapter. L.W. Carr was named chairman, but by the next meeting, the chairman was Dumont Peck. In June of that year, a great campaign for the War Fund was made with

$15,500 as the goal. Teams went door-to-door, suppers were given (at 25¢ a meal), the Boy Scouts recruited to help, and the chapter collected $18,061. First aid classes were given and Waveland, New Market, and Mace women formed sewing circles. By September that year, the local chapter was almost 500 strong. In 1920, the local chapter hired Marie Michaels as its first secretary. In 1927, a Junior Red Cross was started. In 1930, Lurena Thompkins was named executive secretary. A disaster plan was created by George Ecker. The Red Cross helped local folks who had hard times during the Depression years. During World War II, the local Red Cross added blood drives, home nursing, and canteen services among other aid. The office moved from the Ben Hur Building to the city hall; in 1963, to a duplex on Water Street; and in 1974, to a home purchased from the Pearl Kelly Wells estate. Longtime Red Cross volunteer Bernice Wray would get up at 4 a.m., make an urn of coffee, stop off for donuts, and go to the post office basement to wait for a new batch of "boys" to leave for the war. She said, "Red Cross has done a lot of good for a lot of people and I'm so proud of my part of it." Velma Keesling, executive secretary for 22 years, recently retired. Mark Franklin is the current head of the local Red Cross.

Music? Of course, the Athens of Indiana needs music and, in the spring of 1891, Josephine Stilwell (affectionately referred to as "Miss Josie" by her friends) approached fellow music teacher Mrs. A.B. Anderson and asked if she'd be interested in helping create a Crawfordsville Music Club. Miss Josie had gone to the State Music Teachers Association convention and had come back inspired that

Situated at 113 South Water, across from the main fire station, the local Red Cross unit began in 1917.

it was a necessity to find a way to share the singing and playing of music in our city. That summer, another friend, Martha Hall, took Miss Josie and Mrs. Anderson around with her horse and carriage in order to talk to the musical ladies of the city. As a result, 22 women attended the first meeting. According to an article by Becky Groves in the February 1984 *Montgomery*, the name Musical Amateurs was adopted. The first concert was presented in early November of that year.

Beethoven was the center of attraction and the ladies not only gave a paper about the man's work, but presented several of his pieces as well. Printed programs provided the outline of each program through 1932. The February 18, 1892 *Crawfordsville Journal* stated the following:

> What was probably the most artistic and classical home talent concert in the history of Crawfordsville was given last night at Music Hall [Strand Theatre] by the Musical Amateurs. Every number was executed with an elegance and correctness which excited the admiration of the large audience.

Miss Josie kept a scrapbook of the group for over 40 years. By 1922, the group had grown to 575. According to Groves's article, Henry Campbell, an old Civil War soldier, was the first man to perform for the Musical Amateurs. The group joined the National—and newly organized Indiana—Federations of Music Clubs that same year. The next year, the group felt that their old name was outdated and chose Crawfordsville Music Club instead. Mrs. Robert Tinsley was elected the first president of the new group and also the first vice president of the Indiana Federation

The state Grand Army of the Republic met here for a grand gala in 1909.

of Music Clubs in 1924. The group recruited youngsters and had a children's musical in 1926, with performers such as Barbara Bushong, Opal Fruits Early, and Julia Gregg Beemer. Another year an all-men's program was presented with Herbert Morrison as chairman. Groves stated that the Depression "wreaked havoc" with the Crawfordsville Music Club. People dropped from the roles, and money wasn't available for a meeting place. Mrs. Louis Hopkins became a member about this time and she made it possible (her husband being Wabash College's president) to meet in the old Wabash College Chapel in Center Hall. Miss Josie was guest speaker at the 45th anniversary of the group, but died a couple of years later. Her obituary stated that she was one of Crawfordsville's most outstanding women.

Another of the city's older organizations is the Crawfordsville Art League. Twelve women became charter members of the first league in 1896. Mrs. Frank Abraham was the instigator of the group and she was joined by friends Mrs. Hugh Kingery, Miss Mary Grubb, Mrs. John Gilbert, Mrs. A.A. Sprague, Mrs. Harmon Sutton, Miss Sally Harney, Miss Julia Warner, Mrs. Ella Webster, Mrs. Georgia Bodine, Miss May Taylor, and Miss Agnes Schultz. Mrs. Kingery was elected first president. In Jean William's 100th anniversary article about the group, she noted,

> Mrs. Kingery was a remarkable woman who did a great deal to promote arts and crafts in Crawfordsville. The first exhibition was held in Wabash College's Yandes Hall. The prices were interesting: $4 for a water color vs. $125 for an oil painting, but not all of the items were for sale.

Although the league was started by women, men joined and were often made honorary members.

The Current Events Club of Crawfordsville was organized two years before the Art League in 1894, but really got underway with President Eliza J. Moffett in the 1896 and 1897 year. It is thanks to Moffett that so many of the early club yearbooks exist today and can be viewed at Crawfordsville District Public Library (CDPL). Mrs. Moffett was the wife of Dr. Thomas Moffett. The Moffetts, as with many prominent Crawfordsvillians, are buried in Oak Hill Cemetery. Mrs. Lew Wallace was an active member of the club and often told anecdotes regarding the general, his life, and works.

This history would be remiss if the Grand Army of the Republic was not mentioned as an early organization. The roster books of the chapter are fascinating. An example of an entry:

> Walter B. Carr, Co. K. 51st Reg't Indiana Volunteer Infantry.
> Enlisted 18 Nov. 1861 Date of Death: 17 April 1913. Bur. Oak Hill.
> Discharged June 1863 joined GAR 25 Sept 1879 age 38. Mustered in
> As Captain Co. 135th Indiana Vol. Inf. In '64 Comrade Carr departed this life
> April 17, 1913 at his late residence on Vance Street in this city of Crawfordsville.

> Funeral services conducted by Rev. Comrade W.H. Fertich at the home—after which
> Post performed ritualistic services and his remains were lain to rest in Oak Hill Cemetery with the "Honors of the Post."

Sadly, another comrade desired to be buried with full rights as well, but was unable to do so as can be seen in this entry:

> William T. Fry Superintendent of Schools, born in Ohio, U.S. Government, Washington D.C. where he departed this life age 69. It was his wish to be buried by the GAR but from some unknown causes was not made known until after his interment.

The McPherson Post GAR dedicated two cannons "in memory of our volunteer soldiers, both living and dead." The guns had been in actual service and were molded from iron dug from the Iron Mountain of Tennessee, in view of three major Civil War battlefields: Lookout Mountain, Missionary Ridge, and Chickamagua. Many county men were in these battles. Captain Henry Talbot was chairman of the committee to secure the cannons. Mayor B.R. Russell and Judge Jere West delivered addresses. There was an active women's group as well, called the GAR McPherson Women's Relief Corp No. 74. As near as can be told, it was in existence from 1887 to 1961. In 1954, they were 142 members strong. These ladies were made of great stock, as invariably they died in their late 80s and 90s.

Many fine youths have been members of 4-H in our county. Our first extension agent was Ralph Chitty. School education about the new club was one of his first goals. He organized the first Farm Boys' Hike, which began on August 2, 1915 at Linnsburg. Samuel Ralston, then governor of Indiana, sent the boys off with an official speech. They hiked about 60 miles and learned much along the way about America's farming arena. They ended up at the Shades State Park. The first home demonstration agent was not until 1945: Anna Schlatter. Virginia Powers Services holds the record for the most years as agent. In the 1940s, downtown was the site for exhibits. The present 4-H site was secured under the guidance of County Extension Agent Gordon Sowers in 1947. In 1958, a girls building opened. In 1963, a spacious building for fruit and vegetable displays was obtained while Mrs. Glen Saidla contributed money for a sheep building. The exhibit hall and horse arena became realities in 1983. 4-H has played a major role in the lives of many Montgomery County youths for 100 years.

"Let's Meet the President" was a series in the local paper during the 1950s. Although its main objective was giving personal glimpses of the presidents of these local organizations (PTAs, United Church Women, League of Women Voters, Coaches Association, Jaycees, Jayshees, Kappa Sigma Phi, K of C, Women's Golf Association, and many more), there can also be gleaned from them a great deal of history of the clubs themselves. All these articles are housed in small scrapbooks in the library's Local History room.

8. CRAWFORDSVILLE IN THE WARS

The Revolutionary War began about 50 years before Montgomery County existed, so it is a pleasure to be connected to nearly 40 Revolutionary War soldiers. Mr. and Mrs. Richard Wills of Crawfordsville Rural Route have spent much time locating Revolutionary War soldiers, as the DAR members have for many years. In the Old Town Cemetery in Crawfordsville, there are at least three Revolutionary soldiers, one being John Boyd, who has no stone. The Wills know that John was born in 1762 and died on October 15, 1824. His wife Elizabeth (Davis) passed many years later. They had at least two sons, James and William. Soon, the Sons of the American Revolution will mark his grave. Also buried in Old Town is James McArthur, born in 1764 in New Jersey, who died here in 1856. James married Rachel Brown and they were the parents of at least 11 children, most of whom dropped the "Mc" from their name. Thomas Mason's birth occurred about 1761, probably in Delaware since he served in Colonel Hall's Delaware Line at age 17. He and wife Mary Dawson had at least 11 children. His last pension was paid on September 8, 1846. It would be good to find more on Samuel Fields, born 1740, who died after 1825 in Crawfordsville, as he was an officer at the Battle of Brandywine.

Lot Fench, who served as a private in the Bedford County, Pennsylvania militia, is buried on the home place that adjoined the Odd Fellows Cemetery on South Grant. In an American Legion list of buried soldiers, Gillis Hitch is also listed as buried in the Odd Fellows Cemetery in Crawfordsville; however, no stone has been found. He was born in Bridge Branch in Sussex County, Delaware in 1758 and served from his native state. Papers state that he died on February 19, 1847 in Montgomery County age 89.

Jacob Miller was the father of at least five children, including William Miller, who built the first log cabin in Crawfordsville and helped establish the Presbyterian church here. William and Jacob are buried side by side in the Old Masonic Cemetery.

Although Jacob Westfall, who was with the George Rogers Clark Expedition according to grandson Frank Mill's biography, is buried in Putnam County, Frank considered him to be one of ours. He, along with the DAR, dedicated a granite stone in Oak Hill Cemetery to Jacob's memory.

There doesn't appear to be as many War of 1812 soldiers buried here. Perhaps it's because that war wasn't the same in magnitude. At least three are buried in Odd Fellows: William Hocum, James B. McCullough, and James Stitt. Oak Hill also has some of our founding fathers: Nathaniel Dunn, Peter Huff, Jonathan Powers, Henry Ristine, and Charles White. At least one man who fought in the Black Hawk War, Elijah Mills, is buried in Old Town.

James Owens and John Powers fought in the Mexican War in the mid-1840s and are buried in Oak Hill. Frank Mills said Second Lieutenant George Powers was "a fine young fellow killed in a runaway accident . . . his body was brought back to Crawfordsville and the funeral services were impressive." Oddly, there seems to be no cemetery stone for this man, but there is one for a John Powers of the Spanish-American War. Mills also said that Lieutenant Allen May came back "covered with glory as colonel." The story went that when May came home from the Mexican War, he brought a Mexican boy with him who was a lasso expert. He provided great entertainment in Crawfordsville. The boy later studied medicine and theology "and both doctored and preached." May was perhaps a brother to Dr. Willis May. Ninety-eight men from Montgomery County fought in this war.

Not surprising in view of Wallace and Lane's relationship with Abraham Lincoln, Montgomery County was ranked among the highest in the state to respond to Lincoln's call for troops at the start of the Civil War. In fact, it is said that when Lew Wallace heard the call for 75,000 volunteers, he threw down his pen and law books and went to defend his country. Mahlon D. Manson, who had gained some fame during the Mexican War, joined Wallace to rally troops to help put down the rebellion. By their third day of working together, a company had been organized and was ready to go into camp. They planned to leave Crawfordsville early on April 18, 1861.

On the day of departure, thousands of Montgomery Countians gathered to see their young men depart. They formed a long line on Green Street, between Market and Main. A copy of the New Testament was given to each man. Our local papers cried: "It was a sad and solemn occasion as fathers bade their sons goodbye with heavy hearts, and mothers held sons close for perhaps the last time." As the train pulled out with their loved ones, those same mothers and fathers slowly walked home.

Similar scenes would be repeated until nearly 3,000 of our county's sons volunteered in their Civil War. There was much volunteerism in this time. A group of young women in Brown Township made bandages and gathered supplies. Older men joined the local Home Guards. Food was prepared in homes, socks and mitts were handmade, and clothing was sent to the supply depot in Indianapolis. Local writer Mary Hannah Krout wrote about the scene at Wabash College. Her house overlooked the shade of the campus:

> The Civil War was in progress and those gifted with a more prophetic vision began to realize that the struggle would be long and bitter. The

General Lew Wallace was equally famous as a writer, lawyer, statesman, and humanitarian, and is shown here with good friend and Indiana poet James Whitcomb Riley.

> county, the town and the college had been heavily drawn upon for volunteers. The class rooms were nearly empty and the treasury was empty. Since classrooms were almost empty, a score or more of the young women, including myself, petitioned the faculty and trustees for admission but were refused.

This of course is still a sore spot with the women of today.

An amazing feat for such a new city was to send five generals to the Civil War. We've discussed our most famous general, Lew Wallace, in earlier chapters. To add to this information, Wallace was appointed Indiana's adjutant general by Governor Morton when Lincoln called for volunteers. Morton asked Wallace to find enough men to create six regiments from Indiana. It took Lew but five days to recruit enough men for 13 regiments. Lew chose to command the 11th Indiana, which was ordered to join troops at Cumberland, Maryland. When their three months' service was completed, the 11th returned to Indianapolis and the men were mustered out. Wallace recruited enough men to go forth again, this time mustering them in for three years. Quoting from *Montgomery County Remembers*: "In the upcoming months, Wallace would take part in three great battles, receive two promotions, be relieved of his command and sent home to Crawfordsville."

It is well-known Crawfordsville lore that many blamed Wallace for being late in getting his divisions to action at the battle of Shiloh. This is unlikely, as Wallace

Having been a captain in the Mexican War, Mahlon D. Manson worked his way up to brigadier general in the Civil War.

had proven himself and his troops in battle and he was never afraid of a fight. According to Crecelius:

> There was Grant's army with its back against an unfordable river; the Confederates were gathering a large force at Corinth, twenty miles away. Grant refused to order his troops to entrench. Sherman made fun of a colonel who suggested that the union forces should send out scouts to see what the enemy was doing. The result was complete surprise, and near disaster for the Union forces.

But, even after Shiloh, Wallace's troops accomplished important military services. Wallace defended Cincinnati and the great heroics by his troops in defending the nation's capitol against General Early's attack helped his name come into a better light. Current research has cleared Wallace's name, anyway.

Another of Crawfordsville's generals was Mahlon D. Manson, born near Piqua, Ohio in 1820. Manson went to work at a very early age due to the loss of his father. This caused him to miss school, but he read with great fervor the rest of his life. He came to Crawfordsville in 1842, where he followed his line of work as a druggist. He had a beautiful Victorian home on West Market Street where the Family Video Store and Dr. Walker's office are today. The home was destroyed in 1963 when Hook's Drug Store (and Applegrove Restaurant) was built. The dining room in the restaurant was named the General Mahlon D. Manson Room and that too has gone by the wayside.

Manson married Caroline Mitchell in May 1850. They had six children. The general loved children, often stopping little ones to shake a hand or pass the time of day. Having been a captain in the 5th Indiana during the Mexican War, Manson was ready for duties in the Civil War. He was assigned as captain to the 10th Indiana, soon reached the rank of major and later lieutenant colonel. He commanded a brigade at the battle of Mill Springs in early 1862 and was soon made brigadier general. At the battle of Resaca, "his command made an assault on the Confederate works with heavy losses," according to Crecelius. It was in this battle that Manson was wounded and he never fully recovered. He left the Civil War in December 1864. This year, he became the Democratic nominee for lieutenant governor, but lost that race. Manson had previous success in politics, having served in the Indiana House of Representatives in the early 1850s. In 1866, he ran for secretary of state, but was again defeated. In 1870, he beat General Lew Wallace in the race for congressman.

In 1875, he was in charge of the arrangements of the new courthouse dedication. The next year, he was elected state auditor and, in 1884, lieutenant governor, but declined the office when he was appointed director of internal revenue for the Lafayette District. He was also a stockholder in the Indiana Fence Company and was one of four (along with Charles Goltra, Benjamin Wasson, and A.F. Ramsey) to start the Citizens State Bank. He was active in the Grand Army of the Republic, the Masons, and the Methodist church. Colonel W.F. Bush and Manson boarded a Monon train in February 1895. The general told Bush he was drowsy, so two seats were pushed together for the his comfort. Soon he was asleep, a sleep from which he never awoke. Bells all around town tolled for his large funeral.

Although Brevet Brigadier General William H. Morgan went to Illinois after the Civil War, he lived in Crawfordsville during the war years and thus is counted as one Crawfordsville's five generals.

A Mexican War veteran, Edward Canby attended Wabash, graduated from West Point, served as a major general, and was later murdered by a Modoc Indian.

William H. Morgan lived in Crawfordsville when he went to the Naval Academy at Annapolis. Graduating from the academy in 1856, he served two years in the Navy, then came back to Crawfordsville. In 1861, he became a captain with Manson in the 10th Indiana. One year later, he had already achieved the rank of colonel and was appointed to command the 25th Indiana. He later commanded the 2nd Brigade, 5th Division of the 16th Corps, with the rank of brigadier general. His troops were at Donelson and Shiloh and the general also took place in the "March to the Sea" campaign. Although Morgan went to Illinois after the war, he is counted as one of our five generals.

One of Montgomery County's most colorful early settlers would certainly have to be Dr. Israel T. Canby, born in 1785 in Upper Marlboro, Maryland. As a young man, he moved to an inherited estate in Kentucky and married Elizabeth Piatt there in 1816. It is not known when Dr. Canby had time for doctoring, as he was heavily into politics, becoming a senator almost immediately after becoming a doctor. Canby lost the race for Indiana's governor in 1828, then switched careers, becoming the United States land officer of Crawfordsville, succeeding Ambrose Whitlock in that job.

There was a Canby addition to Crawfordsville, which was named for this man. Dr. Canby founded the Crawfordsville Female Academy in 1840. One of Dr. and Mrs. Canby's seven children, Edward R.S. Canby, was another of Montgomery County's generals. Edward attended Wabash College for a while, then entered West Point. After graduating there in 1839, he served in the Mexican War. Again, that experience landed him a commission in the Civil War and it wasn't long after its onset that Edward Canby was made major general of volunteers. He continued

General Henry Carrington is not counted as one of Crawfordsville's five Civil War generals, but came here shortly afterwards to serve as military science professor at Wabash College.

to serve in the army after the war. While negotiating with the Modoc Indians on April 12, 1873, he was treacherously murdered by Captain Jack, a renegade leader of that tribe. The old Crawfordsville High School, the present-day Athena Sport and Fitness Center, is on the site of the old Canby home.

A brother-in-law to General Canby was John Hawkins, who also attended Wabash College for two years, then entered West Point.

> After his graduation in 1852, he served on the frontier against the Indians. When the Civil War got underway, he was assigned first to Fremont's then to Grant's command. After serving in the Vicksburg Campaign, he was promoted to Brigadier General and given command of a colored brigade, and for the remainder of the war was stationed in the Louisiana-Arkansas area.

Although technically the Athens city had only the five generals enter the Civil War, General Henry Beebee Carrington came here shortly after the war. Coming from a long line of Yale graduates, Carrington himself graduated with the class of 1845, which sent seven generals to the war. He was an extremely religious gentleman, being quite active in the Presbyterian church. Via an act of Congress, Carrington came to Wabash as a professor of military science. He was a lawyer and member of the United States Supreme Court bar. Quite a prolific writer of essays and speeches, he was much in demand as a speaker. A father of eight children, he also had a brother John who was a lawyer in the city.

In Frank Mills's autobiography, he also listed these Wabash graduates as generals: Joseph J. Reynolds, John C. Black, Charles Croft, and Smith Fry. Wabash provided several colonels, majors, captains, and lieutenants as well.

Another of Crawfordsville's fine Civil War soldiers was Henry H. Talbott. His father Courtney was of Southern gentry, owning many acres and several slaves. However, young Henry fought with great pride for the Union Army, Company C, 7th Kentucky Cavalry. Henry tallied seven battles. He was wounded twice (in the right lung and right leg) and honored twice. During the war, Talbott's family lost much and ended up as farmers in Vigo County, Indiana. In 1872, Captain Talbott married a Waveland girl, Hester Evans, and they moved to Crawfordsville. Talbott organized Crawfordsville's McPherson Post, Grand Army of the Republic, and wrote the National Horse Thief Detective Association secret handbook. Horses were his love and even after many people were driving cars, the captain would ride his favorite horse through the streets of the Athens City. Talbott died in 1931 in his 90th year and is buried in Oak Hill. There were few left in Talbott's GAR group, but 11 members stood at attention while American Legion members fired off a final salute to the old Kentucky gentleman.

Captain William Herron had been attending Wabash College when he enlisted (along with 350 others) for the Civil War. Not yet 18, he was made first sergeant in the 72nd Indiana Volunteers. He served with them until the war ended and was on Sherman's famous March to the Sea. It is said that his division had the honor of capturing Jefferson Davis. He was wounded at the battle of Chickamauga and was discharged in poor physical condition. Unable to work, he again enrolled in Wabash College. In 1868, he began work with the First National Bank. Quite a versatile man, he was president of the first gas company and installed the first gas works. According to an article in *Montgomery County Remembers*, he was on the executive committee, "which directed the erection of the Soldiers' and Sailors' Monument on the Circle at Indianapolis and a member of the Commission erecting the Indiana monument at the Chickamauga battlefield." For many years, he was trustee of the Indiana Home of the Deaf. He worked at the First National Bank, remaining there for nearly 60 years. Sol Tannenbaum replaced Herron, who was then 84 years old. William and his wife Ada had one and only one home, the "gingerbread" house at 406 West Wabash, which was later moved to Pike Street. Herron died in 1927. Many Herron relatives attended Wabash College, including William and Ada's four sons Charles, Frederick, William, and Austin. Charles became a general, serving in both world wars, and was a friend to Dwight D. Eisenhower.

J.W. Ramsay, mayor in 1881, was another Civil War veteran of Crawfordsville. He attended Wabash and studied law under Lane and Lane's partner Wilson. When Ramsay became mayor, Crawfordsville was $20,000 in debt. Under Ramsay's supervision, the debt was liquidated. V.J. Wert, another vet, served three terms as mayor in the early 1900s.

In the July 1999 *Montgomery County Magazine*, Jim and Patience Barnes discovered one of the most interesting and little-known Civil War stories of our area. George W. Riley was a son of James and Margaret. George, along with brothers John and James, attended Wabash College. Almost immediately upon Lincoln's request for Union soldiers, George joined up with Company E, 15th Regiment for a three-year stint. A large pamphlet at the Indiana State Library contains records indicating George's dishonorable discharge. Repeated in Terrell's Adjutant General's Report and Bowen's *History of Montgomery County*, the Barnes's article proves that this was just not true.

About 300 Montgomery County soldiers died in the Civil War, including several who were on their way home when their ship, the *Eclipse*, blew up.

We get a feel for life during the Spanish-American War from Fred Hurt's letters home. The son of Dr. William Johnson and Susan (Thomas) Hurt, Fred attended Wabash College, then studied at the Indiana School of Medicine. While there, he "Tried time after time to go, each time receiving the marble heart," as he put it. When he finally enlisted, he left quickly before changing his mind. "The papers say the health in camp is improving. It's not true. We're allowed 90 men to do jobs in our hospital, but only 14 are able to do duty," he wrote. Hurt remarked

William Herron was attending Wabash College when he enlisted. He was on the executive committee that erected the Soldiers' and Sailor's Monument in Indianapolis and worked at the First National Bank in Crawfordsville for nearly 60 years. The Herron Home is well known to most Crawfordsvillians.

that it was true patriotism to nurse all the soldiers with contagious diseases. He contracted typhoid fever and died on August 28, 1898. Fred's younger brother Paul Thomas Hurt graduated from CHS and then Wabash College in 1909 followed by the Indiana School of Medicine. He served in World War I, after which he practiced medicine until his death in 1949. The family established the Paul T. Hurt Award, given to a deserving freshman at Wabash.

It is interesting to note that, during the Spanish-American War, a Montgomery County Civil War veteran was governor. Pat Cline's *Montgomery County Remembers* article tells us that James Atwell Mount—son of Atwell and Lucinda (Fullenwider) Mount—was one of the most respected governors our state has known. He was born on March 23, 1843. As governor, he inherited a poorly financed situation and the war brought great stress. He said, "At night when I should have been asleep I have remained awake for hours. It is not the actual work of governor that makes the office a hard one but the ever-present responsibility." Mount died two days after he retired and before he could return home to his beloved Montgomery County.

Albert F. Reynolds of Crawfordsville was a member of the group that planted the American flag at the Battle of San Juan Hill, a decisive battle of the war. His daughter Iva, a member of the Spanish-American Auxiliary in 1961, stated, "it is significant that history tells us in 1898, our nation responded promptly and

Our city's American Legion is named for Byron C. Cox, Silver Star Recipient, who was killed in action.

decisively to action against us as compared to today's indecision!" As many as 264 people from the county fought in this war.

J. Harold Wingert was the first Montgomery Countian to die in World War I. He was sent overseas after just four weeks of training and was badly wounded on August 10, 1918. He died the next day. Born in Ladoga on November 20, 1889, Harold's parents were Bailey and Laura (Robinson) Wingert. In 1907, the family moved to Crawfordsville. Harold attended Crawfordsville High School. After the war, his body arrived back in our city. A military funeral brought the Crawfordsville City Band leading the procession with a flag-draped casket to Oak Hill Cemetery.

During World War I, college presidents throughout the United States grew concerned about the decrease in students. Wabash's President George Mackintosh joined others at a meeting at Fort Sheridan in August 1918. The purpose was to develop a body of college men for the military and to prevent the decreasing number of regular college students through indiscriminate volunteering. The result? The Students Army Training Corps (SATC), which was to become an army unit with army pay, food, and equipment with all college expenses paid by the government. The men would be sent to officer training camps as the needs of the service demanded.

The board of trustees at Wabash gave their approval to the plan September 4 of that year. The college would provide regular academic instruction approved by the government, meals of standard army rations, proper sanitary housing, and suitable drill grounds. The government was to provide military instruction, uniforms, and equipment, including cots and blankets, and was to pay to the college $1 per day per man for maintenance. Barracks were constructed immediately. In October when the fall term began, 1,525 regular college and SATC students enrolled. Two companies were without uniforms at Wabash and many of the men could not be housed. The first attempts at feeding these men were poor, but the food was said to get better. Don Thompson's article in the July, 1988 *Montgomery Magazine* stated, "Certainly there was little of the traditional ease of college life in sleeping on hard straw mattresses with 200 other snoring recruits and rolling out early, wakened by the bugle on a frosty October morning."

The frostiness got to many and, at Wabash, there was a bad case of the 1918 flu. After diagnosing the cases, local doctors sent these SATC students home until the epidemic was over. Not until October 24 did the normal activities resume. In November, the units received uniforms. Just as they were looking sharp like a military group should, the word came of the signing of the armistice. There was great turmoil in the barracks. It was difficult to keep order in the camp at this great news. Class attendance dropped and military discipline lagged. The men were given the choice of doing manual labor on campus or attending classes. On December 19, the camp was demobilized. The men were allowed to keep one outfit of army clothes and were given their final pay and discharge papers. There were mixed feelings. Some desired to stay, others went home for good, never to return to Wabash. Excluding the SATC men, Wabash sent 748 people to war and Crawfordsville sent many as well.

Local boy Dr. Leonard Ensminger, who obtained the rank of major during World War I, kept the Crawfordsville papers busy. He kept home folks informed of not only what Army life was like for him personally, but also of some history behind the war and what the French people were like. Edgar Hartley received a Silver Star for his war efforts. Byron Cox received his star posthumously. He was born on December 5, 1899 to Danton and Bertha Cox and was a teacher at Darlington when he enlisted. He was killed in action on July 21, 1918. The Byron C. Cox American Legion Post in Crawfordsville is named in his honor.

Edward Bandel, born in Crawfordsville to Fred Bandel (mayor from 1892 to 1896), served in the U.S. Army Ambulance Service and was listed in the Indiana Book of Merit for showing great courage during the Champagne offense. Charles Douglas Herron, the son of William P. and Ada (Patton) Herron was a graduate of Wabash and West Point. He became a colonel and was decorated for bravery. He married Louise Milligan and they were the parents of William and Louise. Paul McCampbell received the Silver Star and was a Wabash College student when enlisting. Several soldiers of our area were members of the 158th Indiana Regiment. Isaac C. Elston Jr. served as their lieutenant. There is a memorial in the Crawfordsville Park for Company M. Reed Morrow, a marine in the 75th Company, 6th Regiment, was born here on May 5, 1895, the son of John and Metta (Mitchell) Morrow. He married Julia Long and had two sons, Robert and Frank. He was wounded in November 1918 and received a bronze star and three silvers. These are but a few of the brave men who fought from Montgomery County. Although America entered the war late, at least four from here lost their lives.

While our boys were off fighting in World War II, many Montgomery Countians were learning to live with less wheat and little meat. Area housewives learned to bake Victory Bread, made from grains, such as barley, rye, or potato flour, and the American hog became almost as exalted as the American eagle. Official Food News demanded, "No sugar will be permitted to use in the making of vinegar." Public eating places were issued rules such as no bread until after the first course. Newspaper clippings from old *Crawfordsville Journal* reviews of soldiers in World War II are full of wounded (Eugene Lawson three times) and killed (Colonel Arthur Lehman, Army Air Corps Instructor for 21 years and the son of Mrs. J.W. Lehman of Crawfordsville, who was killed in a plane crash near New Guinea).

Still others were decorated; Bill LaFoe received the Army's Meritorious Service Award, George Lowe the Bronze Star. There were promotion announcements (Arthur Lewellen to Radio Tech) and other more unusual happenings. James LaFollette of New Market and Bob McClure of Waveland met in Naples and spent several hours together reminiscing. Several local doctors and nurses served in World War II. Fred Daugherty was a major serving 22 months in the Army Medical Corps. His wife served as head nurse of the front lines in the 5th Army Hospital Unit. Lieutenant Colonel H.C. Wallace was engaged chiefly in surgery, while Major Fred Peacock served as a dental specialist. Virginia Haase, Helen Hubbard, Gail Young, and Ruth Steinkamp were local nurses who served. Several area businesses joined the war efforts, Jeschke Wire supplying almost 100 percent of the manufactured specialty wire to the war efforts. The Crawfordsville Foundry supplied castings to other companies that made machinery to be used in the war. John Cochran, the company's secretary, served 34 months in the Navy.

Crawfordsville's own son, Robert D. Weliver, was born on August 30, 1922. He married Arthella Caster in 1946. They celebrated 55 years together. Many will remember that General Weliver's beautiful brick house at 616 E. Main had a howitzer in its yard. Weliver fought in World War II in the Asiatic-Pacific campaign and earned a Purple Heart, three Bronze Stars, and many other meritorious medals. He was a local businessman as well, owning Weliver Trucking for about 50 years. It was a sad day for Crawfordsville when General Weliver was laid to rest in July 2001.

Another Crawfordsville general was history teacher Carl DeBard. He had moved to the city in 1930 and was in the Indiana National Guard until called to active duty during World War II. He received a Bronze Star. In 1954, he was promoted to major general and served as commanding general to the 38th Division for six years before retiring to Ocala, Florida where he died in 1984. A current general, Richard Chastain, still lives in the Crawfordsville area.

Ten Montgomery County boys lost their lives in Vietnam: Harold Abbott, Carl Alexander, Sam Benge, William Clawson, John Corwin, Delbert Haase, Sam Howard, Richard Lynch, Leonard Stalkner, and Lloyd Tribbett. Today, there is an active Vietnam Veterans Association in the area. A current project spearheaded by Tobey Herzog is to tape interviews with Korean and Vietnam veterans.

With Operation Desert Storm fresh in the minds of Montgomery County folks, the September 11, 2001 terrorist attack took place on the World Trade Center in New York City. Several from our Guard units were sent.

Various organizations hold these men in honor, such as the American Legion and the Veterans of Foreign Wars. Crawfordsville citizens should be proud of all these men, who fought to save the freedom of the Athens of Indiana.

9. Tracks to Town

The first "tracks" to town were the old Native American paths followed by crude dirt roads. In fact, three main roads that brought settlers to town existed in the early years. These were Terre Haute, Indianapolis, and Madison Roads. An article by Wilma Shortz says, "The roads were primitive and the going difficult even in good weather. They were little more than trails, neither graded nor graveled, with logs laid as a base in swampy sections." She went on to say, "A horse, a canoe, slow oxen or a man's own legs were to be the only means of transportation for a long time to come."

Isaac C. Elston served as the first postmaster, announcing mail service as early as 1831. A mail wagon went out once a week, going to Lafayette, Covington, and Greencastle. Supplies were purchased in larger cities, such as Cincinnati, Buffalo, Louisville, and Chicago, and hauled back to Crawfordsville by oxen, although some went downriver and upstream via the Wabash and Sugar Creek. Complaints were lodged about the roads in the county. All roads were rough terrain during the rainy seasons. A highway of sorts, laid out in 1845, went from Lafayette to Indianapolis by way of the Athens of Indiana with stagecoaches traveling as fast as 5 miles per hour.

On October 24, 1854, the *Crawfordsville Locomotive* reported the following:

> Ours is perhaps the muddiest town this side of Jordan, and the poet must have had our streets in mind when he wrote the beautiful ballad entitled, "Jordan is a Hard Road to Travel."

Ten years later, it was considered that there was no improvement as a citizen in a local paper complained, "We have the deepest, muddiest, most uncomfortable mud imaginable." Some covered bridges were built (Sperry, Yountsville, Darlington, Deer's Mill, Ladoga, Wingate, and Harshbarger) in Montgomery, but none equal in number to Parke County.

Demands of county commissioners were sought and, in 1877, residents held a major meeting asking for gravel roads. Several roads were leading into the city by 1880, including three "toll" roads. About this time, a tax was levied for the building and maintenance of roads. More roads were built at the cost of $1,200

The first known horse show in Crawfordsville was in 1931. The Athens Saddle Club houses many area horses and often has shows.

per mile. The horse was still an important commodity at this time, as was pointed out by Shortz. In fact, more than 1,698 horses were birthed in the county in 1889. Almost 14,000 horses showed up in the 1900 census. About 1,500 more showed up in 1910, the all-time high. Of course, the horse wasn't just used for hauling; it was utilized for farm work, for hire, to deliver mail and schoolchildren, and for play and show. The first known horse show in Crawfordsville was conducted in July 1931. John Walters and Everett Pavey were the directors of about 100 entries and prizes totaled about $300. Horses are often still seen around the area at the Athens Saddle Club on the Boulevard, the Ben Hur Saddle Club, and the annual (since 1962) 4-H Horse and Pony Show. Of course, for our pioneer ancestors, the horse was replaced by the tractor, cars, trucks, and the railroad.

According to a June 1990 article, as early as Christmas 1831, a committee desired a railroad to be built from Indianapolis to Crawfordsville. Resolutions stated that the members of the meeting were fully impressed with the importance of railroads because they afforded the best means for commercial shipping. The next resolution stated that the group wasn't quite ready to petition for a railroad at this place as "we confidentially believe that our town will be embraced in some of the routes already in contemplation." C.S. Bryant, Isaac C. Elston, and Jonathan W. Powers were appointed to look into the matter further.

In October 1834, a newly formed company, the Indiana-Lafayette Railroad, offered stock for sale and, in 1836, Indiana adopted an internal improvement bill to establish a network of canals, railroads, and roads all over the state. The 1837 Panic slowed things down. In the early 1840s, the real "railroad fever" took place; it wasn't until 1852, however, that the first train came from Lafayette to Crawfordsville. The whole town was there to see it come through, yet it was in the year 1856 when the citizens really got aroused. They were frustrated that

Train travel was big in the city, especially in the late 1800s. The Big Four had four trains daily, while the Monon and Vandalia each had three.

Greencastle was going to take over as a "commercial corporation" large enough to "humble the Athens of Indiana." So tracks to town were coming; however, the 1857 economic panic and the Civil War delayed railroads.

At the close of the war, only one road, the Monon, was available to Crawfordsville residents. Again, the Elstons came through for the town, as Major Isaac C. Elston was a mover and shaker for a line to connect Crawfordsville and Indianapolis. The road was completed in 1869. This later became a part of the Big Four Railroad.

The Logansport, Crawfordsville, and Southwestern Railroad came into the county in 1873. This became known as the Vandalia, while the Louisville, New Albany, and Chicago came to be the Monon. In 1875, a diary stated, "The city has three railroads, giving six different directions of railroad transportation. These roads have constructed a very fine Union Depot at the Junction about one mile from the City." An edition of the *Alamo* paper stated, "Sugar Creek assured Crawfordsville of an unlimited water supply and the community has more railroad facilities than any place in the state except Indianapolis." And they wonder why we're called the "Athens of Indiana?" The Big Four had four trains daily in each direction; the Monon and Vandalia both ran three. The AI&St.L Route (the Midland) "had a late start and an early ending," according to an article in *Montgomery County Legend & Lore*. Although "work on the right-of-way began in 1853, the tracks didn't reach Ladoga until 1887. Browns Valley in '88 and finally, Waveland in 1890." The Monon line was the first railroad to become dieselized.

By 1910, there were few places in the continental United States not easily reached from Crawfordsville. A total of 144.2 miles of railroads stretched across Montgomery County and there were between 18 and 20 steam trains per day in all directions. Three railroads crossed at a junction house in the southwest part of town: the Monon from Chicago to Louisville, the Vandalia branch of the Pennsylvania Railroad from Terre Haute to South Bend, and the Peoria & Eastern Division of the New York Central from Indianapolis to Peoria, Illinois. All three roads had switch tracks, coal dumps, turntables, water tanks, and storage facilities here.

Thousands of passengers passed through Crawfordsville, some staying the night (50¢ for a room with about 24 rooms available), while others awaited another train. It usually wasn't a long wait, as a passenger train passed the junction at least every half hour, day or night. A restaurant took care of the hungry. In an interview tape, Anna Armantrout (wife of Alonzo) remarked, "The wife and daughter of the proprietor waited on customers in black silk and white lace collars and cuffs." Some of the famous folks known to have arrived by rail in the city were James Whitcomb Riley, George Ade, Jimmy Durante, and William Jennings Bryan. In the early fall of 1967, Crawfordsville saw the last passenger train go through its community—the Northbound Monon. CSX was in this area for awhile as well. Passenger service resumed later with Conrail.

The interurban trains, according to the above article, "forever changed the living pattern of Hoosiers." Although the city fathers didn't particularly care for the idea of an interurban, the people desired it greatly and 1,000 city residents petitioned the mayor to get the show on the road. By 1904, there were two hourly passenger lines from Indianapolis to Lafayette and three hourly ones from Lebanon.

The power plant for the Interurban stood across Sugar Creek from today's Elston Ball Park for many years. According to a *Montgomery County Magazine* article by Gary Quigg, "The power plant was a remarkable example of early 20th century technology in design, construction, and operation. With fireproofing in mind, the building was composed entirely of brick, mortar, concrete and steel." Its roof was slate and its symbol of success was the 175-foot smokestack. Four huge boilers were fed coal by hand—this provided horsepower for steam engines, the engines being connected to a 700-kilowatt generator. Automatic oil switches controlled the outgoing high-tension lines. In 1907, the Indianapolis, Crawfordsville and Western Traction Company was organized with $2 million in stock and became known as the Ben Hur Line. Only Ohio had more interurban lines than Indiana during these years.

In 1912, the Terre Haute, Indianapolis & Eastern Traction Company bought out Ben Hur. Stocks and bonds dropped rapidly during World War I and the automobile became popular at this time. On October 17, 1930, the lines closed without advance notice to the nearly 200 people who worked there. The power plant stood vacant for six years until the local Coca-Cola Bottling Company bought and used it from 1938 to 1966. For some time, canoes were manufactured there. The Elston Bank, along with the Department of Housing and Urban Development and concerned citizens, did save the building from destruction and deeded the property for what became Elston Park. State Road 43 was opened into Crawfordsville just three days after the close of the traction line on November 1, 1930. A local streetcar service called the "Yellow Peril," which had started in 1912, continued until 1933 when the automobile took over in most instances of transportation.

Another form of transportation popular in the 1930s through 1950s were taxicabs. The two main companies were the Red Cab Company and United Yellow Cab. Red Cab's instigator was Buck Little and wife Josephine (Duncan). Buck took his one and only car, an old Plymouth, out to his backyard and painted it red on the first day of December 1944. By 1958, the Littles had three vehicles and later five. Cabs ran 24 hours a day, 7 days a week. The rate was 25¢ per passenger anywhere in town. In 1960, the fare was 50¢. Many cab riders were R.R. Donnelley workers. The busiest days were the snowy ones. Four-wheel drive didn't exist in those days, but the heavy cabs with chains got through most any weather. Wally Stewart, owner of Red Cab in 1977 and 1978, said that it was exciting driving through a blizzard. A regular Yellow Cab rider kept calling the Red Cab Company. She was told that they were taking their own customers and emergencies first. Her answer? "This is an emergency! I have to get my hair done." The charge for a ride was $1 and the Sunshine Van was giving rides for a nickel at this time. Insurance was outrageous, so there was little profit in the cab business. Frank Weliver owned the Sommer Cab Company in the late 1930s.

Paul "Pinkie" and Margaret Edwards ran the Yellow Cab Company during this time. Pinkie was quite jovial and he loved his customers. His hours were mainly 6 a.m. to 6 p.m, but regular customers would be picked up at other hours. Although they ran only two cabs, another one "limped around" and was used for backup. At one time, Pinkie owned two companies, the Yellow and the Checker. For some years, the Yellow Cab was in the Illini-Swallow Company, so there were built-in customers. Joe Grabman owned the Yellow Cab in the mid-1940s and often toted old folks for free. He had his own gas tank at his home and was the first to try tubeless tires, according to a July 1948 newspaper article. Joe's son Jerry said, "Taxis were the necessary items," as they were cheap rides. Families seldom had more than one car—if they had one at all—few ladies could drive, and people wanted to get around.

Of course, "hacks" (taxis) go back much farther in Crawfordsville than the Red and Yellow, dating back at least to 1895 when C.O. McFarland's Hack Line existed. In 1905, there were 14 transfer lines, but many of these were horse and carriage for hire for moving furniture, for example.

In 1914, the Crawfordsville Transfer Company at 121 East Market Street, run by John Vanarsdall, advertised, "We meet the train . . . prompt service . . . careful drivers!" Today, there are two companies, Ben Hur and Helping Hand, as well as two limousine services, Elston Grove and VIP. The city of Crawfordsville had a bus line in the 1950s. Martha Lewellen said it was jokingly called the CBB&FE (City Bus, Back and Forth Empty).

The Good Brothers Bus Company began in September 1922. Their first advertisement read, "A bus line has started between Montezuma and Rockville, making four trips a day. Pretty soon, you can travel all over Indiana by bus—providing the roads hold out." It was but a few months later when a new line went to Crawfordsville twice a day. Soon, the brothers purchased a second bus and added more trips. Word of mouth, the sight of a large bus appearing in town, printed time cards, and a schedule printed in area papers let folks know when the buses arrived and departed. Mike and George Good soon realized that the most profitable run was to Indianapolis and, in June 1924, they sold their Rockville to Crawfordsville route to the Ben Hur Bus Company (out of Terre Haute).

In October of the next year, Red Ball Lines purchased Good's Crawfordsville-to-Ladoga section and established a new route from Waveland to Roachdale to North Salem, Danville, and finally Indianapolis. Each bus cost between $300 to $500. Federal taxes for each were $20 with state tax just $5 and city tax $2 less than federal. Insurance for fire and theft was $94 a year, with another $31 a month for property and personal liability. Bus fare one way to Indianapolis was $1.65. Although running a bus line wasn't all velvet, the Good Brothers loved most everything about it. When Mike died in 1954, George continued the bus business for a few years, then sold out, partly because he missed his "Good" brother.

Today, public transportation mostly consists of the Sunshine Van for older folks. The only public passenger train is Amtrak. Sadly, as this book goes to press, there is some talk that this will soon cease as well.

The Crawfordsville division of the Indianapolis, Crawfordsville & Western closed in 1930 without notifying its 200-plus workers. From 1938 to 1966, the local Coca-Cola Bottling used the IC&W power plant.

10. Literary Styles

This chapter is *not* beginning with a Wallace, a Lane, or any famous Montgomery County man; instead, it begins with a lesser-known Crawfordsville gal, Maurine Dallas Watkins, playwright. Information about Maurine comes from an article in the March 1983 *Montgomery County Remembers* by John Elliott of Portland, Oregon, a playwright himself. Maurine graduated from Crawfordsville in 1914. She was an honor student and attended Butler, Radcliffe, Hamilton, Transylvania, and Yale Colleges. While attending Yale, she wrote "Chicago." The vaudeville musical of the same name was based on her original script. Although she wrote articles, reviews, short stories, plays, and screenplays, after 1940 she spent her life in quiet solitude until her death in Jacksonville, Florida in 1969. She never married. At the time of the article, Elliott was completing information for a biography on Watkins. Two other Crawfordsvillians, Kenyon Nicholson and Catherine Clugston, wrote plays for Broadway about the same time.

Another of our little-known writers was Minetta Taylor. Born in Princeton, Missouri on March 2, 1860, her parents (both doctors) were somewhat nomadic. Two of Minetta's brothers, Henry William and John Newton, were Crawfordsville doctors. All three of the Taylors were exceptional writers. Although not of literary subject matter, it is interesting to note that Dr. John Taylor was much too old to have been in World War I (having been born on Halloween, 1849 in Virginia), but nonetheless volunteered his service in any possible capacity.

Minetta Taylor attended DePauw. She was a member of about 30 clubs, even serving as the Indiana state president of the Federation of Women's Clubs. Her obituary stated, "she turned her attention to literature with such success that in a short time she ranked high among the writers of Indiana. Soon, she was in request as a lecturer on literary, social, and political topics of a reform character." She also served as the president of the Western Association of Writers. One newspaper article stated that "there were between 25 and 30 languages spoken in Indianapolis and Miss Taylor was the only person in the state who could talk with practically all of the speakers of these various tongues in their own language." Minetta stated that she could fluently speak 22 languages, read 4 others, and hold limited conversations in at least 7 more. She co-authored six Spanish-English textbooks. She edited the first Kappa Kappa Gamma magazine, *The Golden Key*, published

Crawfordsville doctor John W. Taylor (1849–1935) was president of the Indiana State Board of Health.

in May 1882. Mary Hannah Krout wrote of Miss Taylor's poetry: "it may be classed amongst the finest examples of verse written by an American writer. Her untimely death was an irreparable loss to Indiana literature." She died on July 26, 1911 from a prolonged illness.

You might think it odd to find doctors in the literary section, but several of our county doctors were prolifically talented—Joseph P. Russell, father of nine and experienced early surgeon, was active in several organizations and, in his spare time, enjoyed writing poetry. He died in Waveland on Lincoln's birthday in 1893. Dr. James McClelland studied literature at Miami University in Oxford, Ohio. At least two of his uncles were also doctors, James and Alfred. His paper on milk sickness (a prominent killing disease at the time) to the Indiana Medical Society in 1853 helped save lives in our area. Joining the Civil War, he became inspector general of the Field Hospital in Tennessee. He was discharged due to injury in 1863. He died on August 29, 1875 due to those war injuries. The large, brick medieval-looking home at 602 Cherry Street was built by Dr. McClelland (and was later lived in by another doctor, Preston Layne). The good doctor truly loved to write and many of his poems and articles appeared in various magazines and newspapers.

Writer-doctor Ryland T. Brown led quite an interesting life. He attended the first free school west of the Alleghenies. He exhumed a Native American's body to use as a model in studying bones. He acted as a guide for land seekers. Brown was a minister of the Campbellite Church, strongly against slavery, "vehemently against intemperance," and was chair of the Natural Science Department at Butler, professor of chemistry in the Indiana Medical College, chief chemist in the Agricultural Department under James Garfield, father of six, and author of a "widely renowned textbook" on physiology. Perhaps his best feat is that his daughter Caroline was the mother of the very famous Krout sisters.

Caroline, named for her mother, wrote the novels *Knights in Fustian* (a story of Civil War Copperheads in Indiana), *Bold Robin and His Forest Rangers* (a short story collection for children), *Dionis of the White Veil* (a story of Jesuit missionaries in Indiana), and *On the Wea Trail*. The Wea story shows her love of Native American lore in the Vincennes area during the Revolutionary War. Caroline taught in Crawfordsville, then worked in a Chicago library, but came home because of her poor health, as well as her desire to write.

Her Wea Trail story was of the same subject matter and was a similar story to Maurice Thompson's *Alice of Old Vincennes*. When Caroline discovered this, she was not going to continue with her book, but Thompson wrote her a letter insisting she continue with her work. Caroline wrote stories for Chicago newspapers and for well-known magazines, such as *Cosmopolitan*. For awhile, she served as court reporter for Montgomery County. Caroline wrote under her mother's maiden name, but never owned the drive and confidence her elder sister Mary Hannah had.

Dr. Ryland T. Brown wrote textbooks and was a minister of the Campbellite Church. He was against slavery and intemperance. He was also the grandfather of two exceptional writers, sisters Caroline and Mary Hannah Krout.

Mary Hannah Krout, in comparison, craved the limelight. She was a popular feminist speaker, traveling all over the world. She picked up ideas and purchased a "veritable museum of souvenirs" (tapestries, candlesticks, and a stone from the Great Wall of China). Krout was sent as a correspondent to Hawaii at the time of the abdication of Queen Lilikalana and wrote of political and economic conditions there. From this experience came her book *Hawaii and a Revolution*. Mary Hannah was likely the first and perhaps only nineteenth-century female editor of the *Crawfordsville Journal*, a post she held for three years. As a member of the editorial staff of the *Chicago Inter Ocean*, she was privileged to cover a personal family friend's presidential campaign, Indiana's own Benjamin Harrison. She worked for the *New York Tribune* and *Denver Times*. In fact, it could probably be said that she was a trail blazer for women in the newspaper business.

Mary Hannah Krout began her life on November 3, 1851. She attended school at the Young Ladies Seminary and even attended science classes at Wabash College. While still in school, she wrote a poem entitled "Little Brown Hands." This was a reflection of a harrowing experience when everyone in her family was deathly sick but herself: "Little Brown Hands drive home the cows . . . toss new hay." After appearing in the local paper, the poem was released in the publication *Our Young Folks*. The poem later appeared in school readers. Not only Krout but Lizzie Boynton (who married William Harbert, 1868 Wabash graduate) and others contributed articles to *The Wabash*, and were much loved by the boys. Mary Hannah taught for several years before her writing carried her into the limelight. As a public speaker, few surpassed her. She actually wrote an article for an Indianapolis paper in the 1870s titled "The Hoosier Athens." Mary Hannah Krout died May 31, 1927 and is buried with many famous Crawfordsvillians in Oak Hill Cemetery. Just a walk through this beautiful, hilled burial place takes you on a journey with city pioneers.

Janet Lambert was born in Crawfordsville and it has been speculated that part of the reason she grew up to become a well-known author was her relationships with famous Crawfordsville writers. She went to tea with Mary Hannah Krout. She sat under Lew Wallace's beech tree where portions of *Ben-Hur* were written and watched Wallace paint, and she met James Whitcomb Riley while he visited town. However, being an author was not Janet's first choice of career. Encouraged by her father, she truly desired to become an actress. Sadly, her father died when Janet was 12; thus, her aspiration for the stage was sought alone. Janet's mother sent her to college in Red Forrest, Illinois, but she promptly quit, moved to Indianapolis, and studied drama under a Mrs. Ornsby.

According to Liz Leonard's article on Lambert in the August 1994 *Montgomery County Magazine*:

> One evening she went to see a Whiteside Touring Company play. She was enchanted by the star Walker Whiteside. She was so sure that she could give a better performance than his current ingénue that she went backstage and told him so.

Although she didn't get that part, Whiteside was impressed with the little ball of fire and, in the fall of that year, she received a wire saying, "Come at once!" in regards to a new play. The closing town for Janet's first season was Crawfordsville. Her one big wish was to have a curtain call with the star of the show. Somehow, Whiteside sensed her wish, pulled her out onto the stage, and handed her a bouquet of long-stemmed red roses. The audience burst into wild cheers and Janet Lambert became a star in her hometown.

In the fall of 1917, when Janet was again on tour and at a New York hotel, the phone rang with a voice from her hometown. It was her future husband, Captain Kent Lambert. After a whirlwind romance, they were married and as Kent was leaving for his European tour of service, Janet found out that she was with child. Jeanne Ann was seven months old when Kent returned. Jeanne wrote a wonderful article about her mother in the September 2002 *Montgomery*. Janet found herself caught up in the duties of being an officer's wife, as well as a mother, and her acting days were gone. She became quite astute at playing bridge and wrote several hours a day. "Finally it became obvious either the bridge or the writing had to go, so the bridge went," according to Jeanne Ann's article. Janet wrote various things such as poetry, short stories, and articles. One week after her daughter was married, her first book was sold. A total of 54 teenaged books came from Janet's pen and Crawfordsville tallied another fine author!

One of the most prominent male writers of Crawfordsville was Maurice Thompson. Although not a Crawfordsville native, having been born in the South, Thompson nonetheless considered himself a Crawfordsvillian. Thompson joked about his first publication in this way:

> The Civil War had left me a rather bewildered bit of jetsam stranded on the shore of poverty . . . the thought came into my head that I might write a novel and get money for it . . . I sailed into the task . . . when the story "The League of the Gudaloupe" was finished, I felt sure that I had made a mighty fine story, but somehow the editors and publishers did not see into its wonderful qualities . . . a year or more dragged past . . . some good angel directed me to offer my firstling to the *New York Weekly* . . . in a few days a letter reached me, bearing a check for $100 . . . I was famous and rich.

Oddly, it was 20 years later before the story finally made the press. Thompson wrote, "I had forgotten its title and I could not recall the name of a single character." Obviously, he did not consider it one of his best works, but he did become an accomplished and distinguished writer. Lew Wallace wrote of Thompson:

> Maurice never lost his student ways, not even when a lawyer. His education was everlasting going on, himself his teacher; and that I think

> one of the bonds between us. Success as a writer of prose and poetry was his; but not all of him; he became a Latin scholar and knew the literature of France, like a Frenchman. Still . . . he grew an all-around man, lawyer, politician, geologist, engineer . . . a genius, in short.

His *Alice of Old Vincennes* became a bestseller. Thompson was elected the first president of the Western Association of Writers in 1886. He wintered in Bay St. Louis, Mississippi and summered in Crawfordsville, where he often entertained well-known authors. In 1900, Wabash College conferred the honorary degree of Doctor of Literature upon Thompson. After a lingering illness, he died at his home in Crawfordsville on February 15 the next year.

Born in Montgomery County, Meredith Nicholson became a lawyer, but his interest was writing. He spent several years writing for Indianapolis newspapers before he made his first real money from a published work—$3 for a poem. Shortly thereafter, he received $10 for a short story titled, "The Story of a Postage Stamp." For many years, politics was also an interest and he served as envoy and minister to several countries, including Paraguay, Venezuela, and Nicaragua. After retiring to Indianapolis in 1941; he died there on December 22, 1947.

Although James B. Elmore was basically a son of Alamo, not Crawfordsville, our county would not be the same without his great poetry. He was dubbed "The Bard of Alamo," yet the whole world read his work. Elmore finished high school, but his major desire to attend college never came about. His vast amount of reading gave

Popular teen romance author Janet Lambert grew up in Crawfordsville. She wrote a total of 54 books, many of which are held at the Crawfordsville library.

Prolific Crawfordsville author Meredith Nicholson received $10 for his first short story.

him the ability to begin his life as a schoolteacher. After his marriage to May Ann Murray and the birth of his five children, he decided to invest in some of "God's glorious outdoors" and purchased 80 acres from his father. By the time of the 1913 Bowen's *History of Montgomery County*, he had amassed 540 acres. A member of the Woodmen at Crawfordsville, as well as other fraternal organizations, he spent many years writing poetry, finally gathering his best into books. Most of his poetry dealt with the great outdoors with religious connotations.

Daniel W. Starnes, born in Wallace in Fountain County, Indiana on October 21, 1842, had many "poetic compositions" published in various newspapers and magazines while he lived in the Athens of Indiana. Frank Mayfield was his pen name and his most famous poem under this name was "PawPaw."

Let us not forget the many historical writers of our area, Freddie Bales being the utmost leader of this group. A CHS and Wabash graduate, Freddie died at age 45. He kept his readers interested in the history of our area, while writing a long-going article in the local newspaper. John Bowerman, lifelong resident of our county, did a great service by featuring someone who was a "Profile of Inspiration" in the *Montgomery County Magazine* each month.

While Donald E. Thompson was Montgomery County historian and librarian at Wabash College, he compiled and edited several volumes of *Indiana Authors and Their Books.* Jean, Don's wife, was also county historian for a while and wrote many magazine articles about history. Early Montgomery County history was touted by H.W. Beckwith and A.W. Bowen in their history books. Pat Cline began the *Montgomery County Magazine* and was quite prolific in her county history writings. Gaildene Duncan Hamilton carried on her work for quite some time. The *Montgomery* is still published by the *Journal-Review*, with Tina McGrady as editor. Mike Hall and Joann Spragg have given many insights into the lives of our two famous Crawfordsvillians (Lane and Wallace). Ted Gronert, Dick Banta, Connie Riggs, Martha Cantrell, Bob Wernle, and James Leas, to name a few, have contributed multiple writings in honor of our area.

Of course, it's not just the writers who make us the Athens of Indiana. Probably Crawfordsville's most famous artist would have to be Fritz Schlemmer. Another local artist, Mary Early Johnson, wrote an interesting article about Fritz in *Montgomery County Remembers.* Much of the information about him comes from this source. Ferdinand Louis (Fritz) Schlemmer was born in Crawfordsville on September 26, 1892, the son of Otto and Louise (Miller) Schlemmer, Otto being a successful local businessman. His name is on a downtown building today. Fritz attended Crawfordsville High School, Wabash, and the Chicago Art Institute. Quite an athlete, he played basketball at Wabash and swam while in Chicago. In 1917, Schlemmer was commissioned first lieutenant, 89th Division of the United States Army. After the war, he studied more and began to be in demand for portraits.

He opened a studio over Ecker's bakery on East Main and met Beatrice Deane, who worked at Bischoff's Department Store. He married her two days before Christmas in 1924. They had one daughter, Beverly. Fritz taught art, painted much of Crawfordsville, and was appointed Wabash College's first artist-in-residence. He continued giving lessons to his beloved townspeople, among them Lee Detchon, Peg Shearer, Helen Collar, Betty Dodds, the Domroeses (father and son), Carol Klinger, and Yvonne Kendall. Johnson said, "Schlemmer did murals for Culver Hospital and the city building, judged art shows, and at least one beauty contest at DePauw." Schlemmer died in 1947 of Addison's disease. "His ashes, as he had requested, were scattered over the streams where he had fished!"

Paul McMains was born in Parke County, grew up in Waveland, and spent many years starring as tenor and director of Broadway plays. His talent didn't stop there, as he was also a talented artist. He retired in Crawfordsville. A few current noted painters of our area are Mary Johnson, Jerry Smith, Rob O'Dell, Gene Burns, John Oilar, and Terry Jackson.

Although Dave Gerard laughed off his talent and Dick Banta noted, "The Athens of Indiana is not content with strewing the nation with literary aspirants, it took to plaguing the world with a crop of cartoonists," Gerard nonetheless helped put Crawfordsville on the map with his famous cartoon figure, "Will-Yum." Gerard stated in *Montgomery County Remembers* that among Wabash men and cartoonists were Tom Henderson (who drew zany women),

Bill Holman (Smokey Stover's creator), Paul McCarthy (worked on the Chief Wahoo strip), Frank Beaven (the only one to hit the *New Yorker*), Bandel Linn (magazine cartoons), and others who Gerard laughingly called "The Sugar Crick School of Art."

On this note, this author would be remiss for not mentioning Will Shortz, crossword puzzle guru. Crawfordsvillians are reminded of Will when doing a *New York Times* puzzle or reading *Games* magazine, as Shortz edits both, carrying on our Athens tradition.

Much has been written about Wallace's writing of *Ben-Hur*, so it is fitting to complete this chapter with words from a letter to Lew in regards to the importance of the book on others' lives:

> You have done much . . . for me . . . and I wish to thank you. In 1885, I was a drunkard . . . no future . . . everything was black . . . *Ben-Hur* came into my hands and I read it . . . it brought Christ home to me as nothing else could. I stood up again in the community . . . may God bless you as your book has blessed me and mine!

These writers, artists, actors, and many more we do not have room to name have blessed Crawfordsville.

Lew Wallace's Ben-Hur *furthered Crawfordsville's Athens of Indiana claim. Lew could often be found leaning back in his chair and jotting down thoughts on his "lap top."*

11. THE VALUE OF EDUCATION

A merely adequate education in Crawfordsville has never been acceptable. Foremost on the minds of even the earliest settlers of the city was the fact that advantages could only be gained with an exceptional education. The year 1823 was the birth of the town *and* the birth of its education. Josiah Holbrook held the first school by subscription in a log building that stood in the 300 block of what is now North Washington Street, according to the August 1981 *Montgomery County Magazine*. Eight years later, James C. Scott began the Crawfordsville Seminary, but the offering of only a few elementary courses did not suit our citizens and this school soon went by the wayside. In 1833, Caleb Mills opened what he called the Crawfordsville English and Classical High School. This of course was the forerunner of Wabash College. Mills, a mere 27 years old, welcomed 12 young Indiana boys to the first class. Mills was "professor of language."

Thomas R. Marshall, vice president of the United States from 1913 to 1921, was probably Wabash's most famous graduate. He noted that Mills was one of his best teachers and that "the professors tried to give us some principle of life. They cared not for riches, but implanted the principles in which they believed in the minds of the young men who came under their charge." The first graduating class consisted of two young men, Archibald Allen and Siala Jessup, who received their diplomas on July 11, 1838.

On the evening of September 23 that year, the newest Wabash building caught fire and Mills rushed out to organize a bucket brigade of students and community volunteers. He was inside the building, which had only the floor left, when his blackened face reappeared. For several years beginning in 1846, at the start of the Indiana General Assembly, a series of pamphlets were published urging acts that would set up a public school system. These were compliments of Caleb Mills. In large part due to Mills, the first state superintendent was elected in 1852; Mills was the second in 1854. He returned to Wabash in 1857, where he taught another 15 years, then took charge of the college library.

Young men seeking a secondary school education attended the Wabash Preparatory School and young ladies attended a seminary on Washington Street. This school burned down, but the ladies were well provided for attending classes in the basement of Center Church (on the northwest corner of Pike and Washington Streets). In 1852, the old Canby home was purchased by the Crawfordsville Female Seminary, which had been started three years earlier. This had two buildings, one for the primary grades and the other for the advanced grades.

The following is according to *Montgomery County Legend and Lore*:

> The catalog of 1854 states that written essays were required at least once in two weeks from the advanced classes of the academic department and from all pupils in the collegiate classes. Exercises in reading, spelling and defining, writing, elementary drawing, construction of maps and vocal music will be continued.

There were three school terms per year; each term cost about $6, with extra charges for piano lessons. If an out-of-towner came to the school, the total cost per term was $40, which included board, room, fuel, lights, and tuition. Enrollment soared and, 20 years later, these two buildings were just not enough; thus, the Central Building was built.

In the fall of 1873, 12 rooms housed the school, as well as the superintendent's office. This was a three-story brick building and, in 1880, two wings were added. The original 12 rooms cost $44,000; it is not known how much the additions cost. Mary Brown, Stella Brown, Annie Divine, Jane Krout, Kate Krout, Elizabeth Kennedy, Mary Lewis, Mary Stilwell, and Mary Welty were the first graduating class of 1877. Robert Krout, president of the school board, gave an outstanding commencement address centering on the equality of women. Quite fitting, in view of the fact that he was the father of Caroline and Mary Hannah Krout, illustrious female advocates.

In 1904, two seniors, Walter Harter and Helen Osborne Ristine, combined to write the beautiful song "Gold and Blue." The Old Central School building was used until 1910 until the construction of the building we all know as the Old Crawfordsville High School at 201 East Jefferson Street. According to Bowerman's article, "the new building was literally built around the old structure." Anna Willson was a remarkable principal. All had a vision of greatness for Crawfordsville's schools. "Willson created a system that gained nationwide attention. Per capita attendance ranked near the top for the entire country, and debating, drama and oratory offered opportunities which previously had been nonexistent." She had the full support of Superintendent William A. Millis. His youngest son Robert practiced medicine in Crawfordsville, was president of the city's school board, and produced another city doctor, Sam Millis.

Crawfordsville was the first high school in a large area to offer an honor society. Known as the Nonpareil Society from 1909, it affiliated with the National Honor Society in 1930. In March 1939, the gymnasium with two playing floors was added. Prior to the new Crawfordsville High School, which held its first classes in Fall 1993, football was conducted at Hoover Field. The Gold & Blue section of Lee Whitecotton (and Diane Kreisher's) College Street Pharmacy was a popular

Crawfordsville's Old Central School was used until 1910 when replaced by what we all remember as the old Crawfordsville High School at 201 East Jefferson.

hangout at lunch and after school. The favorite drink was the "Green River," a lime phosphate. Auto Mechanics was in a building on Market Street.

Crawfordsville's high school today has an enrollment of about 700, with Kathy Steele as superintendent and Jeff Henderson as the new principal. There are approximately 40 high schoolteachers. Three grade schools and a kindergarten center educate approximately 1,400. Grades 6 to 8 attend Tuttle Middle School. Dale Petrie is president of the local school board with five members. Sports include cross country, volleyball, soccer, football, tennis, basketball, wrestling, gymnastics, swimming, track, golf, baseball, and softball. Athenian yearbooks can be found in the Local History Room of the Crawfordsville District Public Library.

In Martha Cantrell's article "Unusual School Emerges," she discusses another school in the early days. It was a fine two-story Greek classical frame structure and was not mentioned by either of the two main *Montgomery County Histories* (Bowen and Beckwith). Three famous Crawfordsvillians, William Burbridge, Henry S. Lane, and Chilion Johnson were chosen trustees of the new county seminary in 1837. Property (1 acre) was purchased from brothers Fountain and Yonel Pullen for $32. Johnson, being a carpenter, erected the building and, in the fall of that year, the new seminary was occupiable. It is interesting to note that William Epperson helped Johnson build the school and, although older, took his slate and enrolled, Hugh Wilson being the only teacher.

The new school stood on a hill just north of the Elston Grove. It had white paint and green shutters and was clearly visible to all. John Wilson took over his

Mollie B. Hoover was one of Crawfordsville's finest teachers. She believed "hard work pays off."

brother Hugh's position and the school exceeded the expected population, thus more teachers followed. "By 1849, the seminary began to look dilapidated and was abandoned for school purposes, except for small children who were taught by Mary Galey. The Catholic Church was held in one of the rooms while their house of worship was being built," according to Martha Cantrell's *The Quilt Chronicle*. Although abandoned as an educational facility just 12 years after its beginning, according to the above work, "Within the school's lifetime it was as if the village had left off its crude pioneer façade and was heading pell-mell into the new technological age!"

Born April Fool's Day, 1796, John Beard was quite the advocate for Caleb Mills, yet what Beard did for education was to help establish the free public school system. This occurred by offering an amendment in 1834 to a bill granting a charter to a state bank, which would use surplus monies to establish a free school system in the state of Indiana. Beard died in 1874 and is buried in the Masonic Cemetery in Crawfordsville.

The abovementioned Caleb Mills once stated that an education is, "The birthright of all, without distinction, rank or color." Well, the African Americans of Crawfordsville did indeed have an education, but perhaps not one equal to the whites. In October 1871, it was noted in the *Crawfordsville Weekly Journal* that "the colored school has not yet been provided with a teacher." A month later, "Everything is ready except no teacher can be found." Finally, a few days before

Christmas, the paper noted, "The Colored School is reported in a flourishing condition with James E. Cowan in charge of 36 pupils."

Now, who living in Crawfordsville has not heard of Mollie B. Hoover? Mollie was born on January 22, 1866 to Barnett and Jane (Best) Hoover. The Hoovers had two boys as well, Frank and Fred. The three Hoover men were factory workers and the mother was a homemaker, but that wasn't enough for Mollie. She desired an education and she most certainly wanted to teach children. She did just that for almost 50 years, teaching at the elementary and junior high levels. John Bowerman said that she was typical of the teacher at the turn of the century: "She was precise . . . the t's had to be crossed and the i's had to be dotted."

Mollie almost always had on a white blouse and navy blue skirt. Her Friday quotations "reflected the qualities of ethics, morals and honesty which were so much a part of her life." She believed that hard work paid off. Her goal was to prepare her students for the classes ahead. Mollie died a few days before Christmas in 1933. She left 10 acres of land to "all children, regardless of age, color or economic standing." Twenty-five years after Mollie's death, on Tuesday evening, November 12, 1957, Mrs. Laura Smith, president of the Crawfordsville Board of Education, presented the Mollie B. Hoover School to the community.

According to an article written by Meredith Nicholson, the original campus site of Wabash College was donated by Williamson Dunn. In November 1832, missionary brothers James and John Thomson, along with John M. Ellis, knelt in the snow to bless the ground and the idea of a college in such a small town. The first building was Forest Hall and the first class began with 12 students. Elihu Whittlesey Baldwin graduated from Yale cum laude in 1812, then attended Andover Theological Seminary. He became the first president of the new school. Originally, the name was Wabash Manual Labor College and Teacher's Seminary. Its purpose was to be a classical high school, rising into a college as soon as the wants demanded. Professor Edmund O. Hovey wrote the first catalog.

Upon Baldwin's death, Charles White, a Dartmouth graduate, became president. He was Hovey's brother-in-law. It was somewhat of a question whether White would leave his "interesting, refined and wealthy congregation at Owego [New York]" and come to an infant village. Yet, on "July 19, 1841, students, faculty and citizens of Crawfordsville witnessed his inauguration. During his reign (1841–1861), 131 graduated, 47 becoming ministers, 41 lawyers, 12 physicians, and 9 teachers."

Wabash's third president, Joseph Farrand Tuttle, spent 30 years at the helm. Tuttle was said to have changed very little within those three decades, remaining robust and handsome. His full beard made him easy to spot on campus. Tuttle saw many young Wabash boys go off to war. On most Sunday afternoons, he could be found preaching a sermon in the chapel, with mandatory attendance. The boys were also expected to attend a local church in the morning. Although not a president, Dr. John L. Campbell was easily recognizable on campus and in town. He was a Wabash alumni, principal of the Preparatory School, and on the faculty from 1849 to 1904. He became general secretary for the Nations

The Wabash College Chapel has served as one of the focal points of college and town life for many decades.

Centennial celebration in Philadelphia. He introduced the electric lightbulb to Crawfordsville and worked hard to see that the college and town blended well.

During George Burroughs's time as president (1892–1899), the Preparatory portion of Wabash was abolished, although brush-up courses for college entrants were still in existence for quite some time. He faced quickly-growing enrollments in nearby state colleges and the call of coeducation.

William Patterson Kane, president from 1899 to 1906, was said to have come to Wabash in one of its darkest hours. James Osborne and Ted Gronert wrote that, "the faculty was strong, but student morale was low, the citizens of Crawfordsville unfriendly, irritation over the defeat of coeducation and decline of athletics" were all in existence. In his short time as president, Kane repaired the majority of these problems.

George L. Mackintosh was a widower when he became Wabash's president. He and his son Roderick lived in the big president's house alone. Jean Mitchell Daniels came to aide "Doc Mack" with the housework. On June 17, 1912, much to the delight of college and town, they were married. She spruced up the house and became known for her cheery parties. They had one daughter, Marjorie. In April 1908, the first publication of *The Bachelor* appeared. President Mackintosh was famous for his selection of faculty, including Ezra Pound. A new, undoubtedly brilliant professor, Pound's courtesy to a cold starving girl ("from the burlesque") got him into hot water and he was fired. In 1911, Lawrence "Gippy" Gipson was one of the first of the Rhodes Scholars hired. Wabash is said to have gotten the name "Little Giants" about this time because Wabash was always willing (and able) to tackle colleges twice its size. In 1906 and again in 1911, Wabash was the American Champion in basketball. In 1982, the basketball team became the Division III National College Athletic Association Champs. Mackintosh finished his career in 1926 as president.

During the 1926 to 1940 presidency of Louis Bertram Hopkins, the Alumni Fund and Alumni Council began. Hopkins also upped the level for those entering Wabash. Many gifts were bestowed upon the college by the board and alumni during Hopkins's time.

Frank Hugh Sparks served as chairman of the Education Committee for the Indiana War Commission. A son of John and Jennie (Ryan) Sparks, he was an Indiana native, obtaining his undergrad degree from Butler and doing graduate work at several institutions. Sparks was one of the best-loved Wabash presidents, serving from 1941 to 1956.

Dean Byron Kightly Trippet followed Sparks. Before taking over, the college conferred an honorary doctorate degree upon the new president. Trippet gave Bill Degitz, Myron Phillips, Ben Rogge, and Stephen Kurtz much credit for his presidential successes in his well-written *Wabash On My Mind*. In the year Trippet became president, the college received a historical $1-million contribution. In negotiations with Eli Lilly, a $1-million gift of stocks was obtained (Lilly requested it be anonymous) in order to build a new library. He gave another large sum of money at a later date. Donald E. Thompson served 23 years as the first librarian in the new building, followed by Dick Strawn, and then current

One of Wabash's newest buildings was named for past college president Byron Trippet. A great deal of new construction went on during Trippet's tenure.

librarian Larry J. Frye, who served his 23rd year in 2002. Two of Trippet's accomplishments were the construction of Baxter Hall (largely funded by the Baxter Foundation) and overseeing the building of the Beta Theta Pi House. Others followed. A particularly enjoyable portion of Trippet's book is that of "The Wabash Mystique."

The briefest presidency was that of Paul West Cook, from 1966 to 1968. Thaddeus Seymour followed from 1969 to 1978. Seymour once chose one of the most beautiful fall days, posted signs all over campus stating that classes were cancelled, and read Elmore's poems under the flagstaff. The students loved it!

Lewis Spencer Salter was a Rhodes Scholar who graduated from the University of Oklahoma and Oxford. He was at Wabash College as a physics professor in the 1950s and 1960s, leaving to become vice president of Academic Affairs at Knox College. In 1978, he returned to Crawfordsville to become Wabash's 12th president. Victor Powell, Wabash's speech department chair, served as acting president for one year until Frank Sheldon Wettack came in 1989, staying just four years. He initiated the Forum on Co-Education with the board voting to retain Wabash as a single-sex college.

The current president is Andrew Thomas Ford. His building program has been phenomenal. The Byron Trippet Hall, Allen Athletic Center, Malcolm X Institute, and a new science building have been built or are in the process of being built. The fund has hit the $100-million mark. Ford begins his tenth year as president in 2003.

Wabash creates family legends. Several men of the Ristine family have graduated from Wabash, producing exceptional lawyers, teachers, and politicians. Also, it has been said that families make Wabash a legacy. Some family names with multiple graduates include Bowerman, Boyd, Burhan, Custis, Degitz, Dryer, Engel, Fisher, Forbes, Gorman, Hiatt, Jones, Lehman, Lewis, Lowe, Myers, Powers, Pulver, Rhodehamel, Stout, and Weiland.

Paul Mielke, Paul McKinney, and Vic Powell are the longest-standing members of the faculty at this writing.

Some of Wabash's fraternities are Beta Theta Pi, Phi Delta Theta, Phi Gamma Delta, Delta Tau Delta, Kappa Sigma, Sigma Chi, Lambda Chi Alpha, Tau Kappa Epsilon, Beta Kappa, and Malcolm X. Besides fraternities, there are and have been many clubs in which a Wabash man can become involved, such as Will Hays Republicans, Tom Marshall Club, and Scarlet Masque.

One of Wabash's more interesting graduates was George A. Gordon, born on January 22, 1821. After Wabash, he became a teacher, lawyer, and legislator, being a member of the Indiana Constitutional Convention in 1850. He was the grandson of a Revolutionary War soldier and lived past 103.

Dr. John G. Coulter wrote and edited many "bulletins" to promote the college. Hiram Beckwith, author of the first major county history, hailed from Danville and went to Wabash.

Dr. Walter Fertig, born on June 27, 1917, graduated in the Wabash class of 1938 and taught English there for many years. He contributed many articles to the *Indiana*

Magazine of History and studied the writings, life, and literary career of Maurice Thompson. He aided our Athens community by organizing the Crawfordsville Symphony Orchestra in 1931, which was an active group for several years.

Dick Banta owned a local publishing company for many years. A graduate of CHS and Wabash College, he founded the Wabash publication the "Caveman." His greatest recognition came from a history book, *The Ohio*. We are indebted to him for compiling some of the *Indiana Authors and Their Books*.

Theodore Gronert wrote articles on local history for over two decades in the *Journal-Review*. He was a history professor at Wabash and coached the Little Giant's Tennis Team for some time. He was editor of *Sugar Creek Saga* and co-author of *Wabash College: The First 100 Years*. He did much to preserve Montgomery County history. Many exceptionally written Wabash histories can be found at the college bookstore, the college library, and Crawfordsville District Public Library.

Also at CDPL are histories of the county schools currently being researched and written by Charles Arvin. Don Thompson wrote, "Wabash College graduates have made names for themselves in every field, and on the other hand surrounded by farm dwellers, the city preserves a balance that is unusual among Midwest towns." Thus, whether it be a high school diploma or a college degree, one of the best educations can be obtained in Crawfordsville.

An early scene of Wabash College shows the library and science hall. Wabash's campus is still the most beautiful part of the city.

12. Religion in the City

It wouldn't be wrong to say that the town of Crawfordsville has been built around a belief in God. Two years before the land office opened here, in the summer of 1821, Charles Beatty, a Presbyterian missionary, preached the first sermon heard not only in Crawfordsville, but all of Montgomery County. Wabash College was founded by three Presbyterian men. The First Presbyterian Church was organized in 1824. Two other groups were organized in the 1820s as well, the Baptists and the Methodists.

Reverend James Armstrong, a circuit rider, brought Methodism to the tiny burg of Crawfordsville in the summer of 1825. The idea of a circuit rider can be gleaned during each Strawberry Festival when Dorman Winger appears. After Armstrong's fiery sermons, which he delivered from a tree stump, a few women volunteered to start a class, hoping others would soon become interested. Before 1830, a 40-foot by 40-foot frame church was built on what was then the edge of the southern part of the city (at Wabash "Road" and Water Street).

By 1835, full-time minister Reverend Miller was brought to the congregation. Eight years later, a 20-foot addition was put out on the south end of the church. Oyster ice cream socials, county fair booths, and public lectures brought funding for a new church finished in 1857. Again, in 1886, the church was rebuilt and a large addition added in 1976. Reverend William Graham came to the Methodist pastorship during the Civil War and remarked that there was such great dissension between Confederate and Union sympathizers that only when General Wallace and Senator Lane were home for service was the congregation on civil terms.

The Ladies' Aid Society was active and Mrs. Wallace and Mrs. Lane were supporters. After some changes in names and positions in the women's group, it finally became known as the United Methodist Women in 1967. During Crawfordsville's Centennial, a pageant was staged representing the church's founding. Reverend Lynn Denison just retired and George Plasterer took his place as the current pastor.

On June 10, 1826, a young pastor and his family bought 80 acres of government land 4 miles southwest of Crawfordsville. Michael Combs began having church in his humble log cabin home. In seven years, the trustees of the Christian church decided to move to Crawfordsville. A 40-foot by 60-foot church was built on

At more than 175 years old, the First Christian Church of Crawfordsville is one of the oldest congregations in the city.

Lot No. 40 of the original town plat. By 1855, the church was bulging. Elder J.P. Ewing was beneficial to the new building that was not completed until 1889. In 1903, the chapel area was added, making room for Sunday school. During the 1903 dedication, a pipe organ powered by water flow was given by James K. Everson in memory of his daughter, Sadie. A pageant representing the history of the church, under Reverend James H. Wilson's pastorship, was carried out. The new educational building was built under Miller's time. Reverend Paul Million was pastor for 25 years. Howard F. Miller took over afterwards. The congregation is more than 175 years old.

St. John's, the oldest Episcopal church in Indiana, was founded in 1837. Reverend Malancthon Hoyt was the missionary in charge to build a church. According to a May 1987 *Montgomery* article by Fern Brill, the reverend must have "scurried around a bit to find some leading families who were Episcopalians." The original heads of families making up St. John's were Charles Taylor, Samuel Vance, William Binford, and Thomas Fry. A meeting was held March 7, 1835 and a board of trustees was elected. Mentioned many times in this work, and not an Episcopalian, Ambrose Whitlock was named senior warden, an office he held until 1863. Reverend Hoyt begged the powers to be for a church, as "our greatest difficulty under which we now labor is the want of a convenient place for holding public worship. The County Seminary in which we now meet is nearly a half mile from the settled part of town . . . in winter, the attendance of some is prevented."

Whitlock came to the rescue offering the use of a triangle of land on West Market Street. At a meeting called by Whitlock on March 28, 1836, a committee was formed for the building of the new church and $1,300 raised on the spot.

Construction started right away. Bishop Jackson Kemper, who had approved the church in Crawfordsville and in fact encouraged it, arrived on June 8 "to hold St. John's first confirmation and to lay the cornerstone for the first Episcopal Church in Indiana." For many years, the congregation abhorred the idea of instrumental music. It was the Puritan way to have the priest lead singing, but in 1859, St. John's borrowed a melodian from Lafayette and became the first denomination in Crawfordsville to have instrumental music. In 1872, St. John's members were upset about a saloon across the street, so the church "purchased the Michael D. White property on South Green Street and prepared to move the church to that sight." Thus, St. John's is still strong today and celebrated its 165th anniversary in 2002.

Missionaries from the Lafayette diocese served mass to early Crawfordsvillians, but Catholicism didn't become strong until almost 1860. Irishmen were leaving their homeland due to hunger and the desire for a better life for their families. A group of 12 railroad workers' families put up shanties on the southeast side of Crawfordsville. This shanty town (between College Street and Prospect, and from Wallace Avenue to the Monon tracks) is still often referred to as "Goosenibble." On an empty lot there, the families raised geese. The animals ate anything edible all day long, thus the nickname.

All kinds of social events (weddings, letter readings, and a song fest) took place on the Nibble, according to a *Montgomery* article by Jane Kessler. Irish immigrants usually moved on quickly, but the building of the church gave the community all

St. John's Episcopal Church is the oldest of its denomination in Indiana. Originally built in 1837 on the corner of Market and Water Streets, it later moved to its present location.

the hold they seemed to need. Many of the priests were Irish; the first, Michael Clark, was out of Lafayette. In the early days, the Crawfordsville priests went by hand car to Whitesville and Ladoga. Daniel Maloney replaced Clark and, in the later 1850s, it became apparent that the number of Catholics had so risen that it was necessary to build a church.

Reverend Edward O'Flaherty became the first priest to reside here. Ambrose Whitlock sold three and donated one lot (at the corner of Walnut and North) to the parish. The heavily wooded lot was cleared by parishioners and a 40-foot by 75-foot church with no windows was built, the pews being made from their own walnut trees. Candles lit the church. After O'Flaherty died, Father Maughin reported for duty. His first project was to organize the parish women into an Altar Society. Getting the Holy Cross sisters to begin a school here was quite a feat. They began St. Charles Academy for Girls. The sisters stayed in part of the school. The boys attended school in the church and their classes consisted of reading, writing, math, and religion. The school graduated about half a dozen. Father Maughin believed "there needed to be a strong Catholic Church in a primarily Methodist area." He initiated the first public bazaar. St. Bernard's bazaars have been the highlight of the year for many community folks for decades.

Father Edward Walters purchased the church site at the southeast corner of Pike and Washington Streets. The new church was Gothic style with a large steeple, seating 400. "The altar was donated by Frank Elston, the Protestant Mayor of Crawfordsville," according to a church history by Mark Cain. One of the longest-serving priests was John Dennen. He not only erased the debt for the new church, but redecorated in a "homey" fashion. Civic-minded, he worked for "the betterment of the community, not just his church. Reverend Conroy oversaw the new St. Bernard's school. In June 1937, Joseph Keating came and his "first duty was to buy a house for the nuns." Reverend Henry F. Ward "purchased the 16 acres at 1306 East Main Street." Two of the original stained-glass windows from the old church were incorporated into the new church.

A school was dedicated at the 1306 East Main Street site in 1958. The eight-grade school was closed in 1970 and reopened with the 2000 school year, this time having just kindergarten and first grade with parishioner James Zielinski as principal. It is the plan to add a grade a year through the fifth grade. Suzanne Kalinowski is the 2002 to 2003 principal. The current priest is Melvin Bennett. To make mass convenient for Wabash College students, the Newman Center started in 1967, but closed in 2002.

Trinity Church celebrated its 100th anniversary in 1994. One hundred years before, four clergy—Reverend H.M. Middleton, Reverend J.N. Green, Dr. H.A. Tucker, and Reverend J.G. Stephens—and eight lay people—E.S. Nutt, T.N. Myers, Leroy Miller, D.W. Gerard, George Scaggs, J.N. Zuck, Fred Nichols, and Andrew Yount—met at Yount's home. Several meetings occurred with others joining the original group and, finally, a location on the northeast corner of West Pike and Blair Streets was selected to erect a new church costing $800. The purpose of this church was to serve the growing west end of Crawfordsville.

Seventy charter members formed the new church, which was dedicated on June 9, 1895. The building cost was $7,500. Reverend Stephens was appointed to serve the new church. In January 1968, a new church at 110 South Blair was completed by local contractor Morris Berry. Dr. Phillip Collier is the current pastor.

Just off of Covington Hill, the Church of Jesus Christ of Latter-Day Saints (Mormons) owns a beautiful building. Original meetings were held in the Little House on the Lew Wallace Study grounds. From this humble beginning in the 1960s, about 300 people are now active in the church. If you enjoy genealogy, a Family History Center is located in the church. Tuesday afternoons find Anita Lewis as curator of the research center, Wednesday evening Rolf Samuelsen, and weekends with Steve Thompson by appointment.

The Christ Evangelical Lutheran Church congregation began in September 1956 at Wabash College Chapel with 71 adults and 41 children and organizing pastor John Frank. Reverend Richard Kraus led services, followed by Reverend Rich Graef. Reverend John Stacy got to preach the first sermon in the new church at 300 West South Boulevard just a couple of weeks after his arrival in 1961. A large addition was added in 1976. Christ Church officially became a congregation of the Lutheran Church in America on the first day of the year in 1963. Fifteen years later on the same day, Christ Lutheran became part of the Evangelical Lutheran Church in America.

As early as 1823, the Primitive Baptist Church was organized. From this, a "New School" church was created. In the mid-1830s, William M. Pratt came to our area as a Baptist missionary. To help support himself, he taught school. In 1838, he and 12 members organized the First Baptist Church of Crawfordsville. Early settlers Henry and Nancy (Gray) Ristine were among the charter members, as well as J.B. Austin. Catherine Ashenhurst was the first receiving baptism. A frame building was built by 1843 (corner of Pike and Walnut) on land donated by William Nicholson. It was about this time that Pratt left and an Elder Gray briefly took his place. E.T. Manning was next. By 1866, there were 173 members.

In 1878, the frame church was remodeled. In 1893, a new brick building was built for $99,000. Between 1888 and 1899, the congregation stood at almost 400. In 1897, the local Baptist Young People's group became active. Again, the church was too small and a new cornerstone was laid on October 15, 1915. Much of this church was built by donation; the organ was in memory of William T. Whittington, Elva Whittington, and Mrs. George Manson, and a baptistry was by Kate Rice in memory of her husband Simeon. In the 1930s, 11 young men were ordained ministers and, in 1933, Augusta Hartung was sent to the Congo as a missionary. For several years, the church owned a radio station and broadcast its services in the 1950s and 1960s.

The 1960s brought great things to the church. Politics forced Hartung to leave Africa. This was a plus for the church as she served it for many years, including organizing the Judson Bible Class and establishing the Children's Church. The New Life Singers (for teenagers), under the leadership of Joyce and Joe Fry for many years, were much in demand as inspirational singers. On Sunday, June

8, 1975, the congregation dedicated their new church on Highway 32, east of this city. Pastor James Ranard preached the last sermon in the old church at the site where Crawfordsville Baptists had worshiped for 132 years. Today, the membership is close to 1,000 with about 500 active. Michael Wren is pastor with the Minister of Youth being Michael Rotman.

The First Church of the Nazarene began on July 5, 1920. At one time, the church owned what has been known as the city building across Pike Street at the Lane Place, but most of the early years' worship services were in their North Grant Avenue facility. In 1934, Pastor Grant Barton saw the need for a church in downtown Crawfordsville. They purchased a lot on West Wabash and went to work. With only $1.41 in their treasury, the people built their church, finishing on November 25, 1938. Record Sunday school attendance was 518 students. Michael Uhl is currently their pastor.

On February 11, 1964, people from 15 churches attended a meeting. In May, a charter was opened with 25 people transferring their membership to the new church. When the charter was closed on the last day of that year, 106 members were enrolled. Area ministers preached in the Armory or Christ Lutheran Church until Don Sharp of Hoopeston, Illinois began preaching in May. He moved his family to Crawfordsville in June. A committee was formed to decide upon a site and 21 acres on Indiana 32 east of Crawfordsville were soon purchased. Being built on top of a hill in a wooded area, the new church became known as Woodland Heights Christian Church. The new church was designed for a seating

The church on the corner of Pike and Walnut was the home of the First Baptist Church for over 80 years until the members built a new church on 32 East.

capacity of 500. Church membership at this time was not yet 150. Dedication of the new church was the day after Christmas, 1965. Sharp resigned in 1970 and Lucian Robinson became the new minister.

In 1971, Ralph Swarthout became the first full-time associate minister. In 1974, a new addition was added to the church. The next year, Robinson resigned and Jack Austin followed. In 1978, Del Donaldson became pastoral counselor. Austin resigned after 11 years and Mark Matthews followed for a short time. Ben Wilson came in March 1989 and the church was about filled to capacity. A religion-based preschool began at the church in 1999 to 2000, with Angie Stamper as director. Senior minister Larry Felgenhauer resigned and, currently, Woodland Heights has a membership of 500 with Tony Thomas as minister.

Wick Miller was instrumental in bringing another new church here. Wick is a graduate of Hanover College and did his theological studies at St. Stephens. In June 1995, the Montgomery County Orthodox Christian Association began as a mission of St. Alexis Orthodox Church, Lafayette. Periodic meetings and services were held, but as families were added to the church roster, in November 1997, the bishop of the diocese gave blessings to establish the Holy Transfiguration Orthodox Mission in Crawfordsville. The group meets in the *Journal Review* building.

Methodism in the Crawfordsville area dates back to 1825. The Lane and Wallace families were both active in the First Methodist Church, pictured here.

13. Recreation and Sports

The recreation chapter begins with our public library. On July 29, 1902, the dedication of the Carnegie building took place, with Sue Beck as librarian. Several circulating libraries had provided the borrowing of books prior to this time, but it was the $25,000 gift of tycoon Andrew Carnegie that allowed Crawfordsville to have its public library. Similar to other Carnegie libraries throughout America, Crawfordsville's library seems to have much more charm than most, partially due to the lovely addition added in the 1970s during the directorship of Mary Bishop. Mary Johnson painted the *Alice in Wonderland* characters on the walls of the Children's Room. Marian Powell was the first children's librarian in the room. Currently, Larry Hathaway is the director and Bob Burgess is the board president. Helen Harvey was important in the library's history as she served in many capacities, including children's librarian. Currently, Mary Johnson is working on a history of the library. In the summer of 2002, the library enjoyed an anniversary celebration.

Although once a major means of transportation for our Native Americans and a main highway for our early pioneers, Sugar Creek was also a way of life for millers and today is one of Crawfordsville's unique modes of recreation. As Martha Cantrell pointed out in her *Quilt Chronicles*, Sugar Creek was often used as a "River Jordan," since so many were baptized there in early church services. Sugar Creek also "watered" the elephants in traveling circuses. In 1875, there was a paddle-steamer named *Bessie Turner*. The September 4 issue of the *Saturday Evening Journal* for that year stated the following:

> *Bessie* had been brought back from Troutman's to make trips between Sperry Dam and the Poor Farm every twenty minutes. Beneath her spacious awnings and over her deck, the delightful scenery of Sugar Creek may be enjoyed by tourists.

Neal Watson was the captain. Until about 1890, there were steamers on the creek, but today "modern-day voyageurs" take Sugar Creek canoeing seriously during the annual canoe race. Bob Clements provided canoes for meandering the creek for many years. Sugar Creek is truly one of God's gifts to Montgomery County.

The Crawfordsville District Public Library was dedicated on July 29, 1902 and recently celebrated its 100th birthday. This is an early view of the library.

Another "gift" was our public park. Its gorgeous variety of huge, old trees gives us a taste of how the area may have looked years ago. Harry J. Milligan gave the property for the park to the town in 1911 in honor of his father Joseph Milligan, an early merchant of Crawfordsville. According to an article in the *Quilt Chronicles*, "It was June 14, 1916, before Milligan Park was dedicated," due to the large, several-year project of building roads, erecting a pavilion, creating horseshoe pits, and playgrounds. Another beautiful treed area is of course the grounds of Wabash College. A stroll through either of these grounds brings serenity to the walker.

Many family and class reunions have taken place in Milligan Park. On July 4, 1926, the nation's sesquicentennial was observed by a crowd of 2,500. Old-time tunes were played on a piccolo by Texas Clyde and a great reading of a speech, "The Unknown Soldier," was given by one of the town's outstanding orators, George Beatty. A great blast of noisy and beautiful fireworks ended the program that evening.

Crawfordsville itself was honored in 1965 with its 100th birthday, much of the festivities taking place in Milligan Park. Hundreds of Montgomery Countians took their place in a production called "Sugar Creek Saga."

A great affair was observed on the Fourth of July in 1976. Of course, the annual fireworks concluded the evening as with most Fourth of Julys. In 1991, on the Fourth, citizens celebrated the 75th Anniversary of the park. Family picnics were encouraged. A piccolo player performed, the Woodsmen Quartet sang, and, of course, fireworks rounded out the festivities. The Summer Youth Theatre, under the directorship of Steve Frees, presented "Cinderella," speeches were given by George Beatty, Dr. Sam Kirtley, and Judge Thomas K. Milligan, who ironically is the great-great-nephew of Harry Milligan, the gracious benefactor of our park.

For many years, the Civic Band performed in the shelter in Milligan Park, but has been entertaining groups at the Lane Place in recent years. The band will celebrate its 40th anniversary in 2003. The county music festival with the high school bands performing together was popular for about 55 years.

Emmett Stout, Crawfordsville High School biology teacher in the early 1930s, used the area where Camp Rotary is today for Boy Scout camp-outs. He was instrumental in getting the Rotarians to purchase the property for a scout camp. Two log dams were built on the stream by federal Works Progress Administration employees. The Boy Scouts themselves built bridges and trails through the woods. Stout and his Scouts built the Director's Cabin in 1934 with timber from the camp. Rotarian Al Smith donated a bunkhouse. Other buildings were a mess hall, a cook's cabin, trading post, health lodge, ranger's house, storage building, and a log cabin, also built by the Scouts. The bell came from the Battleship *Minnesota*. In 1985, the 50th Boy Scout Summer Camp was celebrated. In the 1940s, the Girl Scouts began using the camp until Camp Talitha was built at Deer's Mill. The technical name is Montgomery County Youth Camps.

Pat Cline wrote that the Sportsmen's Club has been an attraction to fishermen since it was organized in the early 1930s. Located at 2508 Country Club Road, the club was organized in early 1935 and incorporated on May 31 of that year. Officers at that time were James Kitts, president; T.C. Bell, vice president; and Ernest Ball, secretary-treasurer. The chamber of commerce was behind the project. After the incorporation meeting, the group had a bass fishing contest with Paul Barton winning after catching an 18-inch fish. The most caught was Bud Zeller's 21. After the purchase of 34 acres, a dam 140 feet in length and 22 feet high was constructed. An earthen swimming pool with a 100-foot sand beach was

Among the first staff members of the 1941 Rotary Boy Scout Camp were such surnames as White, Majors, Williams, Guillion, Donaldson, and Toney.

constructed. In Cline's article, Frank Howard acknowledged the many volunteer hours that got the club going. A swimming area was built as WPA and CCC projects. The clubhouse burned down on New Year's Day, 1955. In 1957 to 1958, a new clubhouse was built by the Kirk Quinn Company. The country club dates back to even earlier, 1906.

One of any Crawfordsville teenager's favorite recreation outings was to the Strand Theater, with Andy Browning its longtime proprietor. Sadly, the theater collapsed recently. The old Vanity Theater was deeded to the Sugar Creek Players on December 4, 1983 by Myron Pattison and Ad Vance. The Vanity was built about 1935. The first film shown was *Love in Bloom* with George and Grace, Joe Morrison, and Dixie Lee. Cowboy films starring Roy Rogers and Gene Autry were the specialty. The Vanity closed in 1953. In the 1960s, Wabash's Scarlet Masque enticed play viewers and actors as well. The group had formed in 1971, with Mayor Will Hays as part of the steering committee. In the 1970s, the players began their shows, which are still enjoyed by many community members. The Ben Hur Drive-In holds fond memories for many reading this work as well.

Bowling has always been one of the favorite recreations of the city. Ben Hastings and James Laymon both had alleys on Washington Street in 1900. Older readers might remember the Maple Lane at 110 East Market in the 1940s. The majority reading this work will remember Crawfordsville Lanes on Lafayette Road. Current bowlers go to the Crawfordsville Square Mall. Bowling and other sports trophies can be obtained from Top-Line Athletics. The Sportsman Shop is another place where sports folks like to browse. Other sports such as softball and golf are available for almost everyone.

Shades, Turkey Run, Lake Waveland, KOA, and Raymar provide family camping fun. The Sugar Creek Trail walking path, opened in 2001, is a great place for not only exercising the dog, but yourself as well!

This may shock some readers, but Hoosier Hysteria isn't just synonymous with the Indiana University basketball team. Athenians have had many a fit over the hardwood, too. Basketball in our area began pre-1900 and some historians pinpoint this as the second area to start the sport. The founder of basketball, Dr. James Naismith, had conducted a workshop in his home state of Massachusetts the previous year. Dr. Nicholas McKay, head of our local YMCA, attended Naismith's institute and brought the game back to Crawfordsville so that he might include it in his physical education program.

It is likely that the first scheduled game was on March 16, 1894, between the Lafayette and Crawfordsville YMCA squads, Athenians winning 45 to 21. Number 9 of the original rules of those days was that if a team made three fouls in a row without the opponent having made any, then the opposing team was awarded a goal. There was a referee (ball judge) and an umpire (foul judge). Also, players did not run with the ball, but instead threw it from where it was caught. Although Crawfordsville won the state championship in 1911, one of Crawfordsville High School's most exciting seasons was probably that of 1915 to 1916. The record that year was 26–4, under coach Brandy Freeman. This team was also runner-up

This 1947 photograph by Hirshburg Studios shows a bowling team at the Crawfordsville Bowling Alley at 121 South Washington Street.

for the 1916 state title and had an all-state player, Monte Grimes. Sectional play had started the year before. The game was played at the YMCA and CHS beat New Market 39 to 16 on Friday, March 10. Saturday morning, CHS played Pine Village and won 62 to 27 and trounced Wingate that evening in the final game—score 53 to 9!

From the 16 state sectionals, winning teams went directly to the state final. CHS beat Clinton 40 to 17 on Friday night, March 27. The next day, they beat Kokomo 36 to 21. That evening, in overtime, CHS lost by one point to Lafayette, 27 to 26. Starters for this team were the abovementioned Monte, Paul Manson, Lester Hunt, Clay Bunnel, and Ralph Coffing. Subs were Fred Maxwell and Orville Klendworth. The 1918 to 1919 season was pretty exciting, too. One of the Wingate state tourney players, J.D. Blacker, coached this season for CHS. His record was 30 to 4. Coach Blacker's team beat his alma mater in the first sectional game, 24 to 6. Their next game again kept their opponent in single digits (52 to 4) and, in the final game, 16 to 7 over Darlington. CHS won their first game over Franklin 18 to 14 and their second game 20 to 1 over Logansport, but lost to Lafayette (runners-up to Bloomington in the final game) 18 to 14. This year's players were Don Shelton, Harry Kirby, Maurice Shelly, John Gray, Roy Etter, Maurice Kennedy, Will Gray, Don Montgomery, Maurice Chadwick, and Bob Cadwallader.

From 1915 to 1971, Crawfordsville won the county tourney 33 times. Waveland was next with 12 wins. The fewest points were in 1919 (CHS 16, Darlington 7). The biggest winning margin was in 1957 when Crawfordsville beat New Market

86 to 41 and scored the most points in 1968 with 93 against Waveland's 55. Dick Haslam won the Gimbel Award for scholarship, mental attitude, and basketball excellence in 1958 as an Athenian and later took his Gold and Blue team to five county sectional wins.

Dick Baumgardner coached from 1956 to 1963. He had played at Ft. Leonard Wood, Missouri when the team finished runners-up in the World Army Tourney in 1955, and played on the Illinois and Misssouri State AAU Championships. Under his tutelage, Crawfordsville won five of six sectional titles and, in 1958, was state runner-up. His Crawfordsville coaching record was 105–50. Four Crawfordsville men have served on the board of the Indiana Hall of Fame (established in 1962): Emerson Mutterspaugh as a president, Bob Barton as secretary, and board members Vance Pyle and W. Addington Vance. Some Hall of Fame members from Crawfordsville include Robert Vaughn, David Glascock, Piggy Lambert, Harry Reemann; Maurice Chadwick, Karl Dickerson, and Pat Malaska. Jane Kessler and other Montgomery County Historical Society members had a "Supper of Champions" centering around basketball on April 29, 1988, held at the then-new Northridge Middle School.

We didn't just have high school coaches, we had many marvelous college coaches as well, one being Ward "Piggy" Lambert. Piggy was born in Deadwood, South Dakota, but grew up in Crawfordsville. He was a leading scorer on the

Hoosier Hysteria began with Dr. Nicholas McKay, YMCA head, bringing basketball to Indiana in this downtown Crawfordsville building.

Athenian team (although his adult height would reach only 5 feet 6 inches), starred in basketball, baseball, and football at Wabash, and eventually became a legend in Purdue coaching history. The Lambert Fieldhouse at Purdue is named for our Piggy.

In 2002, unofficial county basketball historian Bob Whalen was working on forming a Montgomery County Basketball Hall of Fame. He is a member of the Indiana Basketball Historical Society and writes wonderful articles on basketball for *Montgomery County Magazine*. Crawfordsville High School does keep a "Hall of Fame" wall, and inducts several to their Athletics Hall of Fame each year. Ralph Wicks, a three-year member of the Crawfordsville basketball team, was termed "the best back court player in the state" his senior year, according to an article in the June 10, 2002 *This Sunday*. The article went on to say that Wicks is also a member of the Wabash College Hall of Fame. Ralph Wilson, class of 1910, was not only a fabulous CHS player, but also showed great promise to be one of Wabash's great athletes; however, he died during a football game his freshman year at the college.

Probably the one player/coach with the most recognition was Pete (Robert) Vaughan. John Bowerman wrote: "Writers across the nation found much to publicize of his college play that earned him All-American. National magazines carried articles concerning his unique methods." *The Saturday Evening Post* gained much from a feature article entitled, "They All Coach At Wabash!" John Bowerman reflected longtime president John Collette of the Wabash Board of Trustee's words, "In my opinion, Pete Vaughan, as a man, stood out even above his accomplishments." Pete's father was part owner of the Vaughan and Casey Bottling Works located on North Green Street, and Pete attended St. Charles Academy, then the old Central High School. Basketball at this point was played at the old YMCA building. Several college coaches worked with high schoolers and vice-versa in the early days of sports. More can be read regarding this great man in many publications, but suffice to say there is a Pete Vaughan Award at Wabash today. Vaughan is a member of the Indiana Hall of Fame, coached at Wabash from 1919–1947, and later served as athletic director, and many still think he sits up on the top row of seats at the stadium.

But there was, and indeed still is, much more entertainment in the Crawfordsville area besides sports. As early as the 1840s plays and circus acts came to the Ramey Hotel, but according to Frank Mills, "For the most part, amusement and entertainment of the city was homemade (singing schools, spelling and geography bees, church socials). A brass band with Ose and Eel Wilhite (local tailors) gave concerts."

Another favorite entertainment in the early times was a dish of ice cream "on the hillside." This was at Yuell Pullen's Chalybeate Springs. Downtown, Yuel had a saloon where he added brandy to his ice cream and called it a "seabreeze." Of course, there have always been favorite fishing spots along Sugar Creek, as well. Major Isaac Elston was said to have been one of Crawfordsville's best at the sport. So, you can see, Crawfordsville has sports. Crawfordsville has the arts. Crawfordsville has great recreation. Crawfordsville *is* the Athens of Indiana.

14. Medicine and Other Happenings

Montgomery County has had an abundance of exceptional doctors. Early physicians rode their horses hard, drove their wagons in hot, muggy Indiana weather, or braved raging streams and winter storms to care for the sick. Few received cash. Most accepted eggs, hens, garden items, and the like for their services. Many early doctors had supplemental jobs, being farmers, teachers, postmasters, druggists, carpenters, wallpaper hangers, printers, a census taker, and even a sea captain.

In the late 1840s, it became apparent to those early doctors that examination and licensing was needed in order to better their profession. In 1849, the Indiana State Medical Society was formed. Montgomery County sent five delegates. In fact, Dr. Thomas Florer served as the newly-formed medical group's first secretary for the next eight years. Montgomery County's Medical Society was not formed until the fall of 1872. At its meeting at the courthouse, Dr. John J. Sloan became the first president. The early doctors (as they are today) were quite civic-minded and most were members of various organizations, such as Masons, Odd Fellows, and local churches.

Dr. Edward H. Cowan served as Montgomery County's first health officer. Several of our doctors, like Cowan, were Wabash College graduates and many had interesting stories surrounding their lives. Thomas Leech loved doctoring, but his real passion was chess. He so adored the game that he played several by sending moves over the telegraph lines.

Elliott Detchon began as a schoolteacher, had medical practices in several places, and upon alighting in Crawfordsville, began the manufacturing of medicines at 213 East Main. His sons Seymour and Irwin aided their father. Interesting articles regarding these patent medicines can be found throughout the area newspapers. One such piece in the February 5, 1881 *Crawfordsville Journal* was as follows:

> One of the best medicines for cough, hoarseness and cold upon the lungs, and as a preventative of lung fever, pleurisy, asthma, bronchitis, croup and all breast and throat complaints, is Dr. E. Detchon's

> Compound Tolu Balsam, for the Throat and Lungs. No family should be without it during the cold and changeable weather of winter.

Dr. Detchon did so well that he built what was considered a mansion at the time on the corner of Wabash and Green. When asked how many rooms his house had, he would say, "Don't know, but I wanted to make sure there was a room for everyone!" Good thing, since there were seven Detchon children. His home—where Walt's Service is today—was a beautiful place.

There were other unique stories as well. "Pleasant" Winston gave greetings to match his name while riding one of his three favorite horses and chewing on a leg of mutton. Dr. Benjamin Briggs performed the first laparotomy (removing a 23-pound tumor) in Montgomery County. If you'd like to read more about the early doctors of the area, read *Montgomery's Medicine Men and Women* published by the Montgomery County Historical Society in 2002.

Often, doctoring seems to be a family affair. In our own time, we can name a few—the Peacock brothers and Marion and Sam Kirtley—but in those early days there were many. Stow Detchon was a cousin of Dr. Elliott Detchon, mentioned above. Frank and John Adkins were brothers. Isaac Newton Brent's father and brother were doctors, and then there's the McClelland family. Albert J. McClelland was the son of Dr. James McClelland. Alfred McClelland's son Dunlap became a doctor (and early funeral director), and Dr. James S. McClelland studied under his uncle James and practiced with his uncle, the above Alfred. James aided one of Montgomery County's few early women doctors as well.

Dr. John J. Sloan was the first president of the Montgomery County Medical Society.

Dr. Elliott Detchon said he did not know how many rooms were in his large house, shown here.

Fanny McClelland read medicine under her uncle James. She graduated from the Eclectic Medical College in Indianapolis. She married James Rich, a farmer. She practiced in our area for 15 years, moved to Frankfort, and then Lafayette. Upon retirement, she moved back to Crawfordsville and ran a boardinghouse on North Grant where she died in 1921.

Another female doctor who ran a boardinghouse (at 224 South Green, according to the 1910 census) was Dr. Martha Hutchings Griffith. She was the only female in her academy class and the youngest member in 1870 when she graduated from the Woman's Medical College in Philadelphia. She was the first woman in Indiana to receive a diploma from a recognized medical college. Her specialty was obstetrics. Her husband Thomas Jefferson Griffith was a Civil War veteran who studied medicine with the above Dr. J.S. McClelland. At the time of his death, Dr. Griffith had practiced medicine in Montgomery County for 54 years and was the last of the charter members of the local medical society. The Griffiths' son, James Barton Griffith, continued his parents' practice.

Another woman specializing in obstetrics was Mary Morrison Hoover. On an 1866 business card, she pleaded, "A share of the public patronage is respectfully solicited." Born in 1829, she married John Hoover, a tinner, at the young age of 19. They lived in Frankfort for a few years, then came to Crawfordsville. At the age of 35, she attended the Cincinnati Eclectic Medical College from whence she graduated. But she didn't stop there. She also graduated from the Woman's Medical College in Pennsylvania. Mary raised two daughters, did her doctoring, and was active in civic affairs. She was especially active in the Presbyterian Church, Daughters of Rebecca, and IOOF. In the 1880 census, she and her family lived on East Wabash and her daughters Mollie and Mattie, along with niece Kate, were all listed as "doctoress."

Another early female doctor, Mary Holloway, was born near Crawfordsville on a cold February day in 1831. Her father Washington Holloway was a cabinet maker. Her mother Elizabeth King died when Mary was 17. Having poor parents, Mary set out to make her own way in life. She sewed, taught, and paid her own tuition to Penn Medical College in Philadelphia. She came back home again to the Athens of Indiana and hung out her sign on Wabash Avenue, where it remained until her death. Quite a woman's activist, she was the chair for organizing the Woman's Suffrage Association and served as the group's first secretary.

At close to 30, she married Eleazer Wilhite, a local tailor. More than ten years older than his wife, the couple still had seven children. Mary loved children. In fact, Dr. Mary is credited as the founder of the Orphan's Home in Montgomery County. Always able to "inspire hope in the sick chamber," but not acceptance from her male colleagues, it wasn't long after her death that these same doctors got together to pay her homage. These words were spoken that day: "By her labors as a physician and humanitarian, she has built a monument more lasting than could be carved on a marble slab or written on a parchment roll . . . and hundreds of people . . . will revere the name of Dr. Mary H. Wilhite."

Basically, it was women who got us our first hospital, which opened in 1902. For several years, a group called the Women's Union had worked hard to "relieve the suffering of the poor classes of Crawfordsville." Mrs. D.C. Smith hosted the first hospital support meeting as early as February 1897. Officers of the group included Mrs. Smith as president, with Mrs. R.E. Bryant, Mrs. F.M. Dice, Mrs. E. Warner, and Mrs. J. Wright serving. Three years later, the group had collected only $54 toward the hospital fund. A public meeting was held in April 1900 with General Lew Wallace requesting support from the community. As much as $1,000 was added to their meager beginnings. To go along with the Woman's Union name, the community agreed that the new hospital should be named Union Hospital. At a later meeting, men got into the act; Charles Travis was named president and other officers were M.B. Thomas, Judge A.D. Thomas, Mrs. L.F. Hornaday, and Mrs. Charles Goltra.

By April 1, 1901, the fund had grown 12 times. The largest single contribution came from Mrs. L.L. Culver with her $10,000 check in memory of her late husband. The name was changed to Culver Union Hospital in honor of the this family. In less than a year, property was purchased and J.M. Bishop, contractor, was procured. Hospital fees were set—$7 per week for ward beds, $10 and $15 for private rooms. This would take care of everything but the doctor's fees. Indigent patients would be cared for by the doctors on a two-month rotating basis. Every doctor in the county was a member of the staff. Edna Humphrey, a Montgomery County native and 1897 graduate of the City Hospital Training School in Indianapolis, was named hospital administrator. One trained nurse and two student nurses joined the staff.

> The new hospital was a colonial style structure situated on the knoll in Whitlock Place between Jones Street and Dubois Avenue. Community organizations (Elks, Tribe of Ben Hur and others) furnished the rooms. Thanksgiving Day was dedication day. Judge West accepted the hospital for the county while Mayor Russell did for the city. Doctor Allhands' sister Hattie Striley of Clinton, Iowa was the first patient.

At the time the hospital was built, it was adequate, but it became a small facility in need of modernizing a few years later. World War I halted the idea of immediate expansion. A decade of discussions among civic and professional leaders slowed the process even more. Finally, on May 12, 1929, the new facility opened. There were accommodations for 48 patient beds. Chairman of the Hospital Board of Trustees was Shirl Herr. Lizzie Goeppinger was superintendent of the hospital. Construction cost $125,000. Health awareness made this building obsolete in just a few years.

A $100,000 improvement came about in January 1941, raising the bed capacity to 85. Almost immediately, it was recognized that this new facility was again too small and, by 1958, there were no private rooms available and beds were even in the hallways. Local architect Carroll Beeson designed wings to the east and south that included 40 additional patient beds, plus an obstetrics area and lab facilities. Dr. Wemple Dodds established the first clinical laboratory in a county-owned hospital during those years.

In 1977, a $500,000 laboratory expansion was completed. About 1981, the county council voted to get out of the hospital business. Non-profit American Medical International was awarded the go-ahead to build a new hospital. In July 1982, Montgomery County became the first in Indiana to sign a lease/sale agreement for hospital care to a for-profit corporation. Longstanding Culver Hospital became AMI (American Medical International) when the new hospital was built in 1984. In November 1999, the name of St. Clare Medical Center was chosen and remains today. St. Clare's has added a dialysis center and neighborhood center. Greg Starnes is CEO of the hospital, which has over 80 physicians on staff, 400 employees, and 160 volunteers with a 120-bed facility. Clinics are the well baby, adult health center, and a diagnostic and surgical center appropriately named "Athens."

15. Crawfordsville for 15 Decades

Chapter One brought Crawfordsville up to about the 1870s, so we will continue from here, highlighting the important happenings throughout the next 15 decades.

One of the city's proudest moments occurred under the leadership of Mayor William H. Laymon. Colonel H.B. Carrington headed a committee to build a new city hall at a cost of $9,000. It was about this time when the city had its first volunteer fire department. Their two engines were named "Niagra" and "Rescue." In April 1874, a new newspaper came into print. This was the *Saturday Evening Journal*, under the directorships of T.H.B. McCain and John Talbot, but in 1888, Talbot left the business and the paper became known as the *Crawfordsville Weekly Journal*.

According to an 1875 geological survey done by state geologist E.T. Cox, Crawfordsville was listed as a "healthy city" because of its "elevated position and natural drainage." The streets were wide and "carefully graded, shaded with native trees to add to the beauty of the city. The residences are neat and tasteful, and wear an air of thrift and comfort. Several manufacturing establishments are prosperous and profitable." There were 59 miles of gravel roads going out of Crawfordsville to county towns. "The total cost for these roads was $88,500, constructed by private corporations, under the gravel road law of 1872." Cox's report went on to state, "The beneficial influence of these roads is great, especially remembered by those who were tortured in their travels 30 years ago."

Although we are all familiar with and most of us have worked at the Strawberry Festival, few know that the first Strawberry Festival held on the lawn of the Lane Place was not the one in 1975, spearheaded by Jane Kessler and Pat Cline, but a much smaller celebration conducted by Joanna Elston Lane herself. She, along with some Methodist church women, charged 10¢ for their strawberries and the festival lasted only a few hours in the summer of 1878. Today, the Strawberry Festival brings thousands to the lawn of Joanna's home and features car and tractor shows, a softball and tennis tourney, children's events, live music, and many interesting craft and food booths for a three-day affair that involves a large part of our community.

That year, the first city directory by James W. Beasley appeared and was well received. In Crawfordsville there were five agricultural implement sales, seven bakeries, two banks (Elston and First National), ten bakers, ten boot and shoe makers, a bottling company, bowling alley, brewer, eleven carpenters, four china and glassware sellers, two carriage and buggy makers, two bookstores, six blacksmiths, six boardinghouses, a bathhouse, seven billiard halls, seven cigar and tobacco stores, four manufacturers (P.L. Fisher, H. Koenig, D. Lanum, and C. Schweitzer), a circulating library, a claims agent, four clothiers, two coal dealers, a coffin factory, five dentists, ten dress makers, six druggists, eleven dry goods businesses, two engravers, the American and U.S. Express Company, three flour mills, a foundry, three furniture stores, five men's clothing stores, four grain dealers, twenty-one grocers, two gunsmiths, three hack lines, two "hair works" shops, three hardware stores, hay press and hay derrick places, five hotels, three house furnishing stores, an ice dealer, eight insurance agents with over forty insurance companies, a machine shop, three marble yards, four meat markets, seven milliners, a music store, three "news depots," six newspapers, twenty-one notary publics, Ramsey & Gilkey Opera House, six painters with eight places selling paint, four photographers, twenty-three physicians, a piano tuner and a piano seller, two picture framers, three planing mills, two plasterers, five printers, a pump manufacturer, two real estate agents, three in the "repair" business, seven restaurants, three saddle and harness places, fourteen saloons, five sash and blind dealers, two sawmills, four seed dealers, a sewing machine agent, a soda water manufacturer, four stave and headings dealers, four stove and tinware places, five tailors, a telegraph company, two undertakers, a U.S. Commission, and three wagon makers. Of course, there was a police and fire department, plus Mayor John R. Coons, twelve churches, six cemeteries, and three railroads.

In January 1879, Maurice and Will Thompson (both writers) held a get-together in Crawfordsville to form the National Archery Association. Representatives from clubs throughout America were here and Maurice was chosen as president. The Thompson brothers are considered to be the fathers of American archery. They were tagged as the Wabash Merry Bowmen. Today, archery clubs are named for them. The 1870s ended with the start of the annual County Fair, organized by the Union Agricultural Association. Dorothy Russo and Thelma Sullivan, in their book *Bibliographical Studies of Seven Authors of Crawfordsville, Indiana*, commented, "It remains an interesting fact that a town with a population of little over 5,000 in 1880, when *Ben Hur* was published could have made this book possible. All Indiana cities, including Indianapolis, must bow to the astounding high rate of scholarship in Crawfordsville."

One of the most unique happenings occurred in 1881. This was the construction of our very unusual "old" jail. This jail was in use for almost 91 years and today seems to be the only jail with working rotating cells. The jail was designed by Indianapolis architects Brown and Hodsgon. The structure contract was awarded to Indianapolis contractors Hinkley and Norris for $15,150 and Benjamin Haugh was to do the ironwork at $10,800; however, the jail was more than $3,000 over

This city hall was built at the price of $9,000. What to do with the bell in its tower caused much controversy in the city.

budget before its completion. Besides the large mechanism and 16 cellblocks, there was a residence, kitchen, back porch, stable, and shed, as well as an engine house, on the premises.

Another first this year for Crawfordsville was the telephone. A crude automatic dial service was available through Central Bell. According to *Montgomery County Legend and Lore*, Home Telephone Company put in another service in 1892. In 1911, Central Union purchased Home and, by 1914, the two systems were made into one.

In 1882, the Indiana State Board of Agriculture held the Farmers Institute at Crawfordsville on March 22 and 23. H.D. Manson greeted those present, and Mayor J.W. Ramsay attended. Many impressive speakers, including James Mount, Professor J. Coulter, Dr. R.T. Brown, and P.S. Kennedy from our area, enlightened the attendees.

Probably one of the most interesting happenings of the 1880s was the murder of Jim and Mary (Matty) McMullen, followed by Montgomery County's first execution. John Coffee, not yet 21, was an only child of a widow, but was reared by the Frank Bagleys, who lived near the childless, middle-aged McMullens. John Coffee had never been in any trouble, but was tagged as slow in the head. Many felt John was not responsible for the McMullen's death. He said that a man named Jim Rankins had invited him to the McMullens' for a party. Rankins told John that it was to be a "chicken roast." John didn't think this odd as the neighbors were always having such get-togethers. He did think it odd, though, when he got to the McMullens and saw that he was the only guest. Shortly after John's arrival, Rankins came in, walked over to Jim McMullen and shot him in the forehead. Coffee said that Rankins forced Matty McMullen to tell where they kept their money. He took it, then doused Matty and the room with kerosene and lit both. When the burnt bodies were removed the next day, the bullethole was easily seen in Jim's head.

John Coffee was arrested for the murders and, on October 16, 1885, he was hanged. The rope was tested for strength by tying it around a big bag of sand weighing 200 pounds, but when Coffee was dropped, the rope broke. In fact, it broke twice. At the second attempt, Coffee started to speak, but was warned to keep silent. The third time, Coffee was pushed off the scaffold. The man who pushed him received $1,000. Many called this blood money as he was stricken by an incurable disease very shortly after Coffee's hanging.

A "sky monster" reportedly appeared over Crawfordsville on April 5, 1891. It was about 18 or 20 feet long, 8 feet wide, and no tail or head was visible. A flaming red eye was noticeable. It squirmed in agony. The *Journal* called it a "mysterious apparition which hovered over our city." Reverend G.W. Switzer, pastor of the

The Ross brothers had the local predecessor of the Dollar General stores. Their 99¢ store was heavily patronized in the late 1800s.

Methodist Episcopal Church, said that he stepped into his backyard at 212 East Wabash to get a drink from his well and there was a strange weird sensation that crept over him. His attention was drawn upward and he beheld something—it puzzled and astonished him. He felt an "unseen force" sweeping toward him. "It was about 16 feet long and eight feet wide, resembling a mass of floating drapery." About two o'clock that morning, Marshall McIntyre and Bill Gray were at the barn of William Martin on East Main hitching horses to their ice wagons. McIntyre's description closely matched Switzer's. V.Q. Irwin said it was a spirit, while Robert Burton called it a delusion. For sure, something was seen over the skies of the city at that time.

Today, everyone loves the Dollar General or Big Lots store, but in 1891, Crawfordsville had a similar shopping store, the Ross Brothers' 99¢ store.

Although the municipal electric plant was organized as early as 1890, production did not begin until two years later. The first plant stood on the northwest corner of Spring and Green Streets. Byron Russell, mayor, appointed E.W. Elmore, James E. Davis, and J.P. Walters as a Light Committee. There were no existing city-owned light plants (previously Crawfordsville Gas Light had been providing some illumination to the city), thus the Athens of Indiana was breaking new ground.

Letters to the editor came out in the newspapers, both pro and con. H.S. Braden went so far as filing a suit against the city. It went all the way to the Supreme Court, but the city won. The *Journal* stated the following:

> Crawfordsville is a city of poles like Indianapolis is a city of churches; Logansport a city of bridges; Lafayette a city of beer. In Crawfordsville there are five or six poles on every corner and five or six in between along with telegraph and telephone ones.

William C. Carr, mayor of the city, said that the purpose was to provide lights for streets, alleys, and public buildings. Thus, on September 9, 1891, guests arrived from Indianapolis, Frankfort, Marion, Rockville, Clinton, and other cities. They toured the city in open carriages, visiting the Wire Fence Company, Water Works, Gas Factory, YMCA, and Wabash College, among other places. The electric plant tour was last, then the group went to the Robbins House for a banquet. Former mayor B.R. Russell was toastmaster for the occasion and said that the event would mark one of the city's proudest days.

Soon, electricity was desired by all and, by January 1910, a movement began to build a new power plant. City residents voted for a new plant, 700 to 75. An article by Pat Cline stated, "The city administration's vision to become a City of Lights continued to move toward fulfillment and on July 3, 1911, the new electric plant began operations and the first juice was sent over the wires that night." In 2002, the manager of the electric facility was Roy Kaser, and board members were Myron Pattison, Tom Sheets, Don Fine, Joe Hinesley, and John Siamas as president. It is thought that Crawfordsville Electric Light and Power is the oldest city-owned electric company in the state.

In 1896, the women of the community made a list of desires for the city that included sewers, good streets, a hospital, a garbage wagon, a street railway system, a carefully selected library, a Woman's Christian Association, ladies vote on temperance, more charity work, more manufacturers, fewer saloons, and Wabash to be co-ed. Except for the latter two, history tells us that our city has accomplished all. About this time, Meredith Nicholson wrote, "There is an ineffable charm about this old town . . . a cultivated society has always existed at Wabash College . . . the town has been called Athens by envious and less favored neighbors."

In the late 1800s, Birch brothers James, John, and William ran the Wabash Machine Works. Their children were all in the business. About 1901, two of these cousins, John Hayes and John Henry Birch, established Birch and Birch Machine Shop. They produced the Little Liz Engines for several years.

There were 6,649 Crawfordsville inhabitants in 1900 and, to begin the new century, Crawfordsville found itself in a frustrated situation. The area had smallpox. There were so many cases by 1901 that a pest house was built on Sugar Creek. Those coming into the city on the Monon train could see it and the doctors sent the extreme cases there in order to try to deter the situation. One doctor went to the high school and gave such a vivid description of the disease that students fainted. Each student thereafter had to bring a vaccination certificate to school or go home. Dr. John Newton Taylor was quite active in getting the children inoculated.

On the Fourth of July in 1901, Crawfordsville had a famous visitor, Carry Nation. J.J. Insley of the Elks sent her the invitation. She wore a black bonnet, linen duster, had a large umbrella and large hatchet, as well as piles of luggage. She stayed at the Crawford Hotel. A parade with about 6,000 in attendance began the celebration. Mayor Charles Elmore introduced her. Interestingly, the stand erected by the Elks fell about 4 feet, but Charley Gilbert broke her fall. Although she did little barhopping (the Elks discouraged it), the event made the year for our city.

Jerre Voris was one of the earliest undertakers in Crawfordsville. His son Samuel Edgar was Crawfordsville's mayor from 1904 to 1910. Sam served in the state legislature after that and one of his major accomplishments was introducing a bill to create penal farms. In 1906, Ralph Schwarz, a well-known sculptor from Indianapolis, designed the Soldier's Monument seen on the southwest corner of the courthouse lot. This was to memorialize all soldiers from our county who fought in any war. In 1909, the local GAR hosted a state encampment.

To usher in 1910, the *Crawfordsville Journal* bragged about what Crawfordsville had to offer: "Crawfordsville has many things which make it desirable as a place of residence and advantageous for the establishment of industries," Among these many things were an orphanage, a juvenile and probation court, ten rural routes, a stone courthouse, a first-class theater, two interurban lines, three competing steam railroads, an artificial ice plant, extensive greenhouses, a paving brick factory, a pressed brick plant, a $65,000 federal building, a hot water heating plant, a modern city hospital, a municipal light plant, a water and gas plant, the handsomest Masonic Temple in Indiana, a beautiful and artistic soldiers' monument, a stone Carnegie Library with 10,000 volumes, a progressive school system with five buildings, four banks and a trust company, The Tribe of Ben Hur, Wabash College with over 300 students, a business college, a commercial club, a civic league, a lettuce farm, an Elks' home, a country club, a machine shop, an iron foundry and match factory, a mitten factory, a casket factory, a bottling works, a healthful climate, two large department stores, the Lew Wallace Study, fraternal and benevolent societies, substantial gravel roads leading to the city, a rich agriculture country, two telephone systems, the most substantial livestock insurance company in the world, the famous Shades of Death Resort, a waterworks system with the purest water in the state, a station of the Standard Oil Company, The Ben-Hur Metal Polish Company, Sugar Creek for fishing and boating, and "the greatest county fair on earth."

The 1910 to 1920 years brought many Chautauquas to the community. In 1912, three-time mayor Dr. Thomas Cooksey was even one of the traveling speakers. Traveling Chautauqua groups operated in the United States from 1903 to 1930, moving from town to town giving lectures, concerts, and recitals. This movement was basically forced out of existence by radio and motion pictures. A huge tent would be set up in a nice location, usually around trees and away from any dusty roads. There would be entertainment for all, with things like "Unknown Australia," a lecture by Kilroy Harris, frontiersman; or a concert by violinist Waldemar Geltch; and for the children, a "Little Lady" harmonica player.

The Masonic Temple is over 100 years old and one of Crawfordsville's most beautiful architectural works.

Much of downtown Crawfordsville was destroyed in the 1933 fire, which smoldered for more than a week.

The year 1913 brought torrential rains to the city, leaving likely the worst recorded flood in our history. Covington Street was like a river. The crest of waves on the floor of Sperry's bridge made traveling unsafe. Even Dry Branch wasn't dry anymore, flooding several neighborhoods.

On May 27, 1914, Crawfordsville had its first-ever Dollar Day. Clothing store owner John Sullivan capitalized on the day in this advertisement: "Mr. Dollar! You have lots of cents when you know your buying power is greater at Sullivan's than any other retail store in Crawfordsville." Early articles in May stated, "the bargains will be the biggest ever!" On Monday, May 25, the paper read, "that old bug-a-boo, the high cost of living, will get an awful set-back on Crawfordsville's Dollar Day. You'll save enough money to start a good-sized bank account." Louis Otto, local jeweler, headed the Dollar Day committee, accompanied by vice president Dumont Peck of the Warner and Peck Mercantile firm. Some bargains priced at $1 were a gallon of paint and a brush, cemetery lot corner stones, cowboy and Indian suits, shirts, and 20 yards of calico.

The Montgomery County Horse Thief Detective Association was quite active in this time as well. In 1915, the county tally was 83, and although there wasn't a Crawfordsville Chapter per se, 26 of these members listed Crawfordsville as their home. In fact, these Crawfordsville men were presidents of the following chapters: Samuel Miller, Linden; William Allen, Hickory Grove; A.S. Douglas,

New Market; Harry Breaks, Black Hawk; Harry Troutman, Yountsville; T.J. Swearingen, Greenwood; J.M. Kessler, Whitesville; Virgil Manuel, Fredericksburg; and J.D. Armantrout, Beech Grove. Twenty-five chapters existed, so few dared to steal a horse.

One of Crawfordsville's all-time great events took place in 1916: the state's centennial celebration. A tablet on the original building of Wabash College was dedicated, a reunion of old teachers occurred, stores closed, there was a parade and historical exhibits, and more than 1,000 actors took part in the Montgomery County Pageant in Crawford's Woods. At 1:30 p.m. on Wednesday June 14, just prior to the pageant, Milligan Park was dedicated. The pageant consisted of three Native American scenes, Surveyors, Offield, Naming of Crawfordsville, Land Sale, Founding of Wabash, Quilting Bee, a Country Dance, Mexican and Civil War soldiers, Caleb Mills, Underground Railroad, Lew Wallace and *Ben-Hur*, Maurice Thompson, and a Grand Finale. Fourteen vets over age 80, one of whom was a woman, Susie Ballard, took special seats. President Taft visited Crawfordsville in October of 1918. His purpose? To promote the Liberty Bond Drive. His host? John Snyder of 201 Wallace Avenue. His speech was delivered at the college.

The Ku Klux Klan was most active in the 1920s. Klansmen marched in local parades. In the summer of 1924, young folks got a bit disruptive throwing firecrackers at the mounted hooded men, however.

The Jeschke Wire Works opened its doors in 1926, making more than 5,000 different types of wire forms. The newest business in 1929 was a toy company, Apex, employing over 100. Also that year, Meredith Nicholson wrote "it would be difficult to find a community more intelligent . . . to know Crawfordsville and its people is to strengthen ones confidence in the future of America."

In 1931, the chamber of commerce put out "Crawfordsville: Athens of Indiana," a pamphlet touting the city. It pointed out:

> Varied industries, ideal labor situation, two railroads, 16 miles of paved streets, power rate of 4 cents a kilowatt, abundant water supply with high pressure, six ward schools and a high school with a corps of 98 teachers, Milligan Park, Crawfordsville Country Club and Municipal Golf Courses, Shades and Turkey Run, Rotary, Kiwanis and the Crawford Hotel, a population of 10,500.

The year 1933 began dramatically, as on January 10 a fire started in the Goodman Department Store. In a short time, a major portion of Green and Main Streets was ablaze. Fire departments from as far away as Frankfort, Indiana and Danville, Illinois came to fight the blaze. Several businesses were completely destroyed with the fire, including C.C. Crist Wallpaper Store, Central Drug Store, Goodmans, J.C. Penneys, Jones Drug Store, Prim's Beauty Shop, S.L. Laurimore's Clothing Store, Schultz Book Store, Security Abstract, Symmes-Williams Electric Company, Tannenbaum Clothing Store, Trask Jewelry, and the Western Union

Telegraph Company. Besides these establishments, many others had second floors or storefronts damaged. The *Journal-Review* had to move to the Strand Theater office to prepare copy, which was set at Indiana Printing. As if the city's worst fire wasn't bad enough, two huge blizzards arrived shortly thereafter, but the Athens of Indiana survived with great effort from its citizens.

Another concern in the 1930s was the bell that was in the top of the Old City Hall on North Green Street, which had been built in 1873. The new building was to be an armory. Carroll Beeson was the architect for the new building, which would be on the opposite end of Green Street. Again, it wasn't the erection of the new building that caught the public's attention. It was the placement of the old bell for more than 60 years. Weighing about 1,300 pounds and being over 3 feet in diameter, the bell had held firmly in the old building, heralding fires, summoning townsfolk to important events, and tolling out the ages of deceased prominent citizens. In a March issue of the *Journal*, it was noted that the bell was to go to the Lane Place lawn, but it is thought it never got there. There was a large bell that stood at the corner of Pike and Water Streets at the city hall property, but it is not known for sure if that was the bell in discussion. There is a large bell at Fire Station 2 today that is thought to be it, and hopefully it will be well taken care of for many years to come.

Crawfordsville was one of the leading centers for milk production in 1941. The Athens City Dairy came into existence shortly thereafter. Louis Schreiner operated the dairy for many years. Ira Clouser was postmaster and Kenneth

Sarah Elliott, with her horse Robin and granddaughter Margie, delivered milk to an early city ice cream parlor.

This old bell now donning Fire Station No. 2 is thought to be the same one that was housed in the old city building for more than 60 years.

Buser his assistant. Maynard Darnell was superintendent of the city schools. Dr. Thomas L. Cooksey was mayor. Lex Clore was the city engineer. Producer's Dairy Products was here for a number of years as well. Stock sales at the Sales Pavilion exceeded $500,000 in this year. Joe and John Binford supplied city residents with lumber and coal. Duckworths gave them competition with lumber and Guy Miles with the coal. Bob Layne for many years had an insulation and roofing business and W.H. Winkler managed the Ramsey Hotel. Mary Callahan was a female optometrist in the Ben Hur Building. Eugene Campbell home-delivered a total of seven newspapers. Myrtle Weathersholt was librarian. Eldon Riggs was manager of Coca-Cola Bottling. After his death, his wife Margaret ran the company.

Another prominent businesswoman was Martha Cowan, manager of a trucking company. For many years, Crawfordsville Paint and Wallpaper aided in sprucing up our homes. B.F. Goodrich was the place to get any kind of tire fixed. Flowers could be purchased from Gould's, Hazel's Bo-Ka Shoppe, Morris & Jack, and Minnie Petts. The Farm Bureau Co-Op in Montgomery County dates back at least to 1941. Noel Shaver had a Hatchery and Feed Store at 122 West Main. American Laundry, owned by Harmon and Helen Shultz, provided a nice service, but several women also laundered in their homes. Inez Cunningham did sewing for many years. Buying clothes at the Golden Rule or Fanny-Bee was a popular shopping excursion. Symmes-Williams was an electric contractor, along with Titus. Telegraphs could be sent via Western Union at 125 North Green. Abstracts could be obtained from Security or Jennison's. Several general contractors existed, including Gus Wray and W.W. Roberts.

Cloverleaf Creameries at 201 South Washington provided yummy ice cream and fountain Cokes. Maplehurst was a later popular place for that. Insurance was provided by William Daseke, Clements, Crawfordsville Trust, Walter Haney, Oscar Stafford, Wright & Quigg, and others. Only 16 doctors were listed in the 1942 City Directory, but there were almost twice as many lawyers, along with 18 churches. Interestingly, two blacksmiths, Mose Feltner and Leotus Wilson, were listed in the city directories as late as the 1940s. Howell-Goodwin and Indiana Printing were prompt in their publishing jobs. The Dobe Inn, Coney Island, Gene's Kitchen, Liter's Café, Speed Grill, and Wilkin's Ben Hur Restaurant were some of the popular eating establishments. Baker's included Clifford Allman, A-Loaf, and Cleveland. Many barbershops and beauty shops existed, as well as a few taverns.

Don Thompson wrote that one of Crawfordsville's famous sons was Joseph "Stephen" Crane, who was born here on February 7, 1916. In the summer of 1942, he met famous Hollywood star Lana Turner at a dinner party. Lana took a liking to him immediately, stating, "By the time he took me home, I was ready to fall in love." Three weeks later, they were married. Crane graduated from CHS

Clark Jones served as mayor in the 1950s. The Crawfordsville District Public Library houses several volumes of Jones's papers and clippings, representing much of the history of the city.

and Wabash College. His father William ran the Stephenson and Crane Cigar Store at 107 South Washington. Steve himself ran the store for a bit. His first marriage was to a local girl, Carol Kurtz. In fact, when Crane married Turner, his divorce was yet to be final. Crane and Turner immediately got an annulment so that he would not be charged with bigamy. In the meantime, Turner discovered she was having a baby, so after his divorce did go through, Turner and Crane finally remarried in Mexico on Valentine's Day, 1943. Their daughter Cheryl was born in July. In October 1943, the two visited his hometown, staying at 215 West Pike. High school students brought their yearbooks to be signed by the famous actress. The Cranes were to stay for five days for a quiet visit, but for some reason, they cut it short. It was thought by local folks that Lana came to Crawfordsville expecting to find richness and found instead a simple, average small-town family. At any rate, she made an impression on the many who trampled the shrubbery around the Crane home to "peek in the windows to see Lana."

Many young male actors had gone to war, so Steve (who did not due to an old knee injury) decided to try his own luck in Hollywood. At $250 a week, he signed his first seven-year contract with Columbia Records. He made only three pictures. However, he found his niche in life in the mid-1940s when he got into the restaurant business. First, he purchased Lucy's, a restaurant near Hollywood that was patronized by movie stars. He purchased others and soon owned six restaurants in southern California, many specializing in Polynesian food. At one point, his revenue was $20 million. Crane died in California on February 5, 1985 and is buried in Oak Hill Cemetery. As per his short marriage to Turner, in an article written by Don Thompson, their daughter Cheryl commented, "She was famous; he was Stephen Who?"

Clark Jones served as Crawfordsville mayor in the late 1940s to mid-1950s. Having previously served as clerk-treasurer, his main goal was to see that Crawfordsville was financially stable. He achieved that. One of his first "accomplishments" was to promote the installation of parking meters. City Attorney Raymond Evans drew up the city ordinance. Fees were 1¢ for 12 minutes, 2¢ for 24, and 5¢ for an hour's parking. This is also about the time one-way streets came into being.

Jones and the Council of Church Women initiated a "World Day of Prayer," here on Friday, February 13, 1948. Jones wrote to several publishing houses requesting "objectionable material not be offered for sale in Crawfordsville." Radio Station WFMU came to town. Later that year, the Lions Club gave away 20 canes to area blind people. During 1948, the city fire department answered a total of 249 alarms. Over $1 million of property was destroyed by fire. Five polio cases in the county were cited at this time and those under 18 were banned by Dr. J.B. Griffith from swimming in the Crawfordsville Country Club and Sportsmen Club as a precautionary measure due to infantile paralysis. The Girl Scout Camp was even cancelled. Jones encouraged citizens to take a new tuberculosis test. The mayor, along with Sheriff Roy Hardaker, targeted the many gambling establishments at the end of the 1940s. Flora Wilson, Horace Mann School principal, received an award from the mayor for the best fire drill. Lester Sommer, president of Crawfordsville Kiwanis, gave the deed to the city's new recreation center on the 400 West Pike Street block.

During this time, the city firemen collected and repaired thousands of toys for the Phi Chi Epsilon sorority's toy drive. In 1950, the fire department received a new emergency unit truck. Women were becoming important to the city's running as Mrs. Noel Shaver and Mrs. Ray Swanson were renamed to the Planning Commission. Mabel Himes was clerk-treasurer.

The 1950 population for the city was 12,804, up from 11,089. On Kiwanis Kids Day, 235 boys and girls participated in the parade. Vance Pyle won the "Pet with the Shortest Tail Award," while Sally Miles took the "Ugliest Doll Award." The *Journal-Review* carriers were taken to Chicago to see the Cubs and Cardinals play. Sewer problems plagued Jones throughout his mayorship and the record-breaking 5.85-inch rainfall in September 1950 didn't help. Harold Walters was appointed the Grade A milk inspector. Walters later became county health officer, as did his son Bob afterwards. Norm McCallum was named director of civil defense. Dave Kadinger held a similar position for many years from the 1960s on.

In 1950, the police made 515 arrests with an 80 percent conviction rate. Several of these were for traffic violations, drunk driving, and disorderly conduct. As many as 1,051 people visited the Lane Place, coming from 30 states, plus Denmark, England, and Canada. Helen Remley served as curator with Walter Remley as president of the board. The A&P Company built a new store at the site of the old Big Four Station that year. Probably the biggest news of 1951 was the drowning of Wabash student Baxter Weber. Faculty members, Red Cross workers, and volunteers all searched for his body in the muddy waters of Sugar Creek for several days until the search was called off. Nine weeks later, the body was found and the remains were buried in his hometown of Olney, Illinois.

Sheriff Remley was hurt in a three-hour siege with a "berserk gunman" on July 20, 1951. The city tax rate was fixed at 1.74 that year. In September, the "downtown street lights were turned on automatically for the first time and the light plant workers joined the International Brotherhood of Electric Workers," according to Jones. A big push was to stop gambling by Prosecutor Beecher Young, who stated he would indeed prosecute anyone continuing gambling procedures. The Eagles, Elks, Moose, VFW, and American Legion immediately removed their machines.

In 1956, the Armory was built. Currently, Lieutenant Colonel Lawrence E. Tipton is commanding officer of the 3rd Battalion, 139th Field Artillery with 13 full-time employees and about 100 guardsmen.

In 1960, Crawfordsville's population totaled 14,000. Dick Ristine was elected lieutenant governor of our state. The year 1965 brought Crawfordsville's Centennial. Ristine was general chairman and the opening speaker. Music was by the Strawn ensemble. Other features included an antique car show, tours of the city's museums, a cast of over 50 in the "Sugar Creek Saga" reproduction, a square dance, band concert, horseshoe pitching, beard contest (William Bonebrake, winner), a parade, and much more. In 1968, the Boulevard Mall Shopping Center opened, bringing with it Bresler's 33 Flavored Ice Cream. In 1969, Mallorys burned with a financial loss of more than $1 million plus 200 jobs lost.

The 1970s brought two tragedies of city employees. Captain Bill (William Henry) King collapsed while fighting an arson-related blaze at the Crawford Hotel. On August 27, 1974, Lieutenant Russ Baldwin was shot and killed when he apprehended a suspect in the robbery of the Grab-It Here Grocery. To honor Russ, a baseball field in Milligan Park was named Baldwin Field. In 1975, Glenn Knecht became the first Democratic mayor in 20 years. Mayor David G. Gerard created a Bicentennial Commission as early as November 1973. Workers for the 1976 celebration included Bill Sikes, Mark Caress, Thad and Polly Seymour, Remley and Eleanor Herr, Jane Kessler, Becky Groves, Max Tannenbaum, David Spohr, Paul Jones, Donis Widener, Marcella Feltner, Russ Miller, and Mr. and Mrs. Lester Sommer. Again, many events highlighted the summer of 1976, including a canoe race, Delta Theta Tau Tour of Homes, Flower Lovers Show, "Arsenic and Old Lace" by the Sugar Creek Players, a dramatic presentation of readings from famous Crawfordsville writers, square dancing, Strawberry Festival, a parade, and much, much more. In 1978, one of the worst blizzards recorded here closed businesses and schools, and caused much damage and even deaths. Linc Priebe hosted the Farm Progress Show in 1979, which brought much business and excitement to our area.

In 1980 a tornado killed one in the county and Amtrak made its first scheduled stop here. In 1982, all of Crawfordsville was excited about native Joe Allen being on a space shuttle. Along this line, Keith Baird, longtime Crawfordsville area physician, was one of the doctors on board the ship that picked up the three surviving Apollo 13 astronauts. The Wabash basketball team won the NCAA Division III Championship. One resident died in a snowstorm in 1985.

In 1969, the Mallory Capacitor Company, a significant area employer, burned, resulting in both great financial and job losses.

In the 1990s, an Amtrak train derailed here. Tornadoes again ripped through the county injuring 12 and making many homeless. The governor declared this a disaster area. The Leadership Academy began during these years. In 1999, a snow/ice storm created school and business closings and cost the road departments $185,000. Also this year, the Capri, an eight-screen movie house, opened in the flourishing Crawfordsville Square.

In 2000, it was pretty exciting to not only bring in a new century, but a new millennium as well. One sad happening was that Crawfordsville had to say goodbye to one of its favorite people. Born in Sullivan County, Indiana on December 11, 1915 (the son of Will "movie czar" Hays and his wife, Helen Thomas), Bill Hays was quite a versatile man. A series on the Hays family can be perused in the 1985 *Montgomery Magazines*. Graduating from Wabash in 1937 and Yale Law School in 1940, Bill served in World War II. Many will remember the "This is Your Life" show hosted by Ralph Edwards. Hays wrote several scripts for the television series. City teacher Ruth Morgan Joiner Thomas was featured on this show for her interesting life. She was instrumental in foiling a Waveland Bank Robbery and was later taken captive in the Michigan City Prison while visiting as a social worker. Hays and his lovely wife Ginny retired to his college town after residing in Beverly Hills for many years. Here he served as one of our mayors. His activities in local affairs included the Wabash Board of Trustees, chamber of commerce, Lilly Endowment, and many others. He authored three books as well. Known as a fine gentleman, Bill Hays's friendly smile is sadly missed in this city.

The year 2002 brought an interesting cultural event to downtown Crawfordsville. The Art League held a regional, juried art exhibit with more than 100 entries. Crawfordsville native Terry Jackson won best of show. In 2002, Les Ingersoll was the city council president. Other councilmen were Les Hearson, Loran Rutledge, Chuck Fiedler, Steve Frees, Darin Hutson, and Neil Barclay. Dave Johnson is police chief and Dennis Weir fire chief. The plan director is Norm Reimondo; Richard Tulley, city attorney; Don McGillen, engineer; Rod Jenkins, street commissioner; and Cheryl Keim, park and recreation director. They head up our beautiful new 26,000-square-foot facility located toward the end of South Boulevard. Under Mayor Steve Gentry's watch, the new police station was built and Random House came to town. On the downside, Crawfordsville has a huge free lunch program and HUD problems. Much is being done, however. For example, the Crawfordsville Chamber of Commerce is making plans to concentrate on downtown revitalization, development of an industrial park, examining the housing market and its impact on local economy, and working to attract jobs 10 percent above national per capita income. Incorporated on February 18, 1918, the group is planning its 85th anniversary celebration in 2003.

I've not found better words to conclude this history than Crawfordsville's own Meredith Nicholson's. He penned, "Crawfordsville's glorious past as a center of sweetness and light lives on in the present." I'd like to add, "and its future!" I hope you enjoyed reading *Crawfordsville: Athens of Indiana* as much as I enjoyed writing it.

BIBLIOGRAPHY

"Abraham Lincoln." *Historic World Leaders*. Detroit, MI: Gale, 1994.

Bales, Freddie. "Thompson's Literary Accomplishments Reviewed." *Montgomery County Magazine*. February 1994.

Banta, R.E. "Crawfordsville Incorporated as Town in 1834." *Montgomery County Magazine*. December 1984.

Barnes, James and Patience. "Restoring the Good Name . . . " *Montgomery County Magazine*. July 1999.

Beckwith, H.W. *History of Montgomery County, Indiana*. Chicago: Beer, 1881.

Blakeslee, Ruth. "The Successful Herron Family." *Montgomery County Remembers*. Crawfordsville: Montgomery County Historical Society, 1976.

Bowen, A.W. *History of Montgomery County, Indiana*. Indianapolis: A.W. Bowen, 1913.

Bowerman, John. "Dr. Dodds Established Clinical Lab at Culver." *Montgomery County Magazine*. March 1984.

———. "Frances Wooden Transformed Lives of Many Youth." *Montgomery County Magazine*. January 1988.

———. "Gerard, Founder of Supreme Tribe of Ben Hur." *Montgomery County Magazine*. February 1984.

———. "Blanche Patterson Left a Rich Legacy." *Montgomery County Magazine*. April 1982.

———. "Freemasonry Has Long, Glorious History." *Montgomery County Magazine*, May 1982.

———. "Holbrook Organized First City School." *Montgomery County Magazine*. August 1981.

———. "Local Teacher's Dream Becomes a Reality." *Montgomery County Magazine*. November 1983.

———. "Pete Vaughan was a Coach's Legend." *Montgomerey County Magazine*. October 1982.

Brelsford, Bridgie. *Indians of Montgomery County, Indiana*. Crawfordsville: Montgomery County Historical Society, 1985.

Brill, Fern. "St. John's Church Celebrating its 150th Year." *Montgomery County Magazine*. May 1987.

Cain, Mark Andrew. "Yesterday and Today: the History of St. Bernard's Church." Crawfordsville: Wabash College, 1986.

Cantrell, Martha. *The Quilt Chronicles*. Crawfordsville: Montgomery County Historical Society and Crawfordsville Art League, 1979.

———. "Unusual School Emerges." *Montgomery County Legend and Lore*. Crawfordsville: Montgomery County Historical Society, 1988.

Cline, Pat "City Council Makes Landmark Decision in 1890." *Montgomery County Magazine*. December 1990.

———. *Crawfordsville: A Pictorial History*. St. Louis, MO: G. Bradley Publishing, 1991.

———. "E.K. Resoner Opens Jewelry Store Here in 1932." *Montgomery County Magazine*. December 1986.

———. "Local Red Cross . . . " *Montgomery County Magazine*. March 1982.

———. "Montgomery Savings Nears Century Mark." *Montgomery County Magazine*. February 1987.

———. "Passenger Trains Stimulated Travel, Economy Nationwide." *Montgomery County Magazine*. June 1982.

———. "Pioneers Start Search for Treasured Land." *Montgomery County Magazine*. January 1983.

———. "Schloot Opened at Crawfordsville in 1933." *Montgomery County Magazine*. May 1987.

———. "Women's Union Fought Hard to get Hospital." *Montgomery County Magazine*. August 1982.

Cole, Evelyn. "Times Have Changed." *Montgomery County Magazine*. June 1990.

Cowen, Janet C. *Crawfordsville Indiana Land Entries*. Indianapolis: Cowen, 1985.

Cox, E.T. *Geological Survey of Indiana, 1875*. Indianapolis: Sentinel Company, 1876.

Crecelius, Owen L. "Crawfordsville's Five Civil War Generals." *Montgomery County Remembers*. Crawfordsville: Montgomery County Historical Society, 1976.

Cumberalis, Glen. "Business, Family Strong Links for Esther Houston." *Montgomery County Magazine*. May 1993.

Cumberalis, Glen. "Gardner: . . . " *Montgomery County Magazine*. October 1992.

Current Events Club Yearbooks. Crawfordsville: Current Event Club, various years.

Dale, John G. *The Golden Era of Montgomery County Basketball*. Crawfordsville: Dale, 1975.

Dean, Jonathan R. "The Construction of the Old Jail, 1881–1887." *Montgomery County Magazine*. August 1998.

Dickey, Roland F. "Lew Wallace: One of Them Literary Fellers." *New Mexico Magazine*. January 1985.

Dictionary of American Biography. Farmington Hills, MI: Gale, 2001.

"Double Murder." *Montgomery County Remembers*. Crawfordsville: Montgomery County Historical Society, 1976.

Elliott, John. "Picking Flowers from the Century Plant." *Montgomery County Magazine*. March 1983.

Encyclopedia of World Biography, Second Edition. Farmington Hills, MI: Gale, 2001.

Family Histories of Montgomery County, Indiana, 1823–1988. Paducah, KY: Turner, 1989.

"Famous Travelers Stopped In City." *Montgomery County Magazine*. December 1981.

"Federal Match Factory Employed Local Women." *Montgomery County Magazine*. November 1988.

Fertig, Walter. "Ristine Had Big Role In College's Growth." *Montgomery County Magazine*. December 1982.

Freedman, Russell. *Lincoln: A Photobiography*. New York: Clarion, 1978.

Gerard, Dave. "The Sugar Crick School of Art." *Montgomery County Remembers*. Crawfordsville: Montgomery County Historical Society, 1976.

Gronert, Ted. "Addiction to Freedom." *Montgomery County Legend and Lore*. Crawfordsville: Montgomery County Historical Society, 1988.

Groves, Becky. "City's Music Club Influential in Community." *Montgomery County Magazine*. February 1984.

Hall, Michael. "The Gift of Our County History." Crawfordsville: Montgomery County Historical Society, 2001.

———. "Henry S. Lane—The Formative Years." *Montgomery County Magazine*. December 1989.

———. "Lane's Burst of Political Ambition Is Examined." *Montgomery County Magazine*. March 1990.

Harvey Robert S. "Montgomery Courthouse Arriving at Centennial." *Montgomery County Remembers*. Crawfordsville: Montgomery County Historical Society, 1976.

———. "These Fleeting Years." Crawfordsville: Wabash College, 1982.

Hill, Dorothy M. "Municipal Airport Became a Reality 30 Years Ago." *Montgomery County Remembers*. Crawfordsville: Montgomery County Historical Society, 1976.

Historic World Leaders. Farmington Hills, MI: Gale, 1994.

Hoyle, Diane. "Giankis Family Operates a Special Shop." *Montgomery County Magazine*. October 1984.

Hunt, Doug. "The Legacy of William Bratton." *Montgomery County Magazine*. 21 February 2002.

Ineman, Kathleen. *The Story of Crawfordsville: 75 Years*. Crawfordsville: R.R. Donnelley & Sons, 1996.

Johnson, Mary Early. *Crawfordsville District Public Library History*. Crawfordsville: Crawfordsville District Public Library, 2002.

———. "Fritz Schlemmer . . . " *Montgomery County Remembers*. Crawfordsville: Montgomery County Historical Society, 1976.

Jones, Clark. "Scrapbooks . . . about his term of Mayor, 8 Volumes."

Crawfordsville: Jones, 1948–1952.

Jones, Marsh. "Prestigious Crawford Hotel Opened in 1900." *Montgomery County Magazine*. February 1984.

Journal of the National Horse Thief Detective Association. Anderson, IN: 55th Session, October 1915.

Journal-Review 150th Anniversary. 14 September 1991.

Kerr, Mildred. "Voris' Thurst . . . " *Montgomery County Magazine*. September 1982.

Kessler, Jane. "Supper of Champions Basketball Homecoming Event." *Montgomery County Magazine*. April 1988.

———. "Irish Settle in Crawfordsville's Goosenibble Area." *Montgomery County Magazine*. March 1994.

"Know your Industries." Crawfordsville: *Journal-Review* (series). 1947.

Krout, Mary H. "Historic Memories Cling to Crawfordsville Lane Place." *Montgomery County Magazine*. July 1994.

Lambert, Janet. "Janet S. Lambert Takes Walk Down Memory Lane." *Montgomery County Magazine*. October 1994.

Leonard, Liz. "The Irrepressible Janet Lambert, A City Native." *Montgomery County Magazine*. August 1994.

"Lincoln, Abraham." *World Book Encyclopedia*. Volume 12. Chicago: World Book, Inc., 1983.

Martin, Marie. "Girl Scout Troops Organized Here in 1920s." *Montgomery County Magazine*. October 1986.

Miller, Wick. "Orthodox Christian Church . . . " *Montgomery County Magazine*. February and March 1998.

Mills, Frank. *Early Days in a College Town*. Sioux City, SD: Sessions Publishing, 1924.

Montgomery County, Indiana. Original entry record book, 1821 and later.

Montgomery County, Indiana United States Censuses. 1850 to 1920.

Morrison, Herbert C. "Banking History Began 122 Years Ago." *Montgomery County Remembers*. Crawfordsville: Montgomery County Historical Society, 1976.

Murphy, Peter W. "Vogel." *Montgomery County Remembers*. Crawfordsville: Montgomery County Historical Society, 1976.

"Newspapers Record Historical Data." *Montgomery County Magazine*. February 1981.

Nicholson, Meredith. "Wabash Connection . . . " *Montgomery County Magazine*. July 1982.

Oilar, John. "Crawfordsville's All-time Coaching Great!" *Montgomery County Magazine*. July 1999.

"Old City Hall Building Razed." *Montgomery County Magazine*. October 1990.

Osborne, James. *Wabash College: First Hundred Years*. Crawfordsville: Banta, 1932.

Phillips, Frank. "Local Policeman is a Friend to Christmas." *Montgomery County Magazine*. April 1999.

———. "Picking Up Speed with Tom Schloot." *Montgomery County Magazine.* February 1999.

———. "Siamas Recalls Wonderful Childhood." *Montgomery County Magazine.* October 1998.

Quigg, Gary. "Interurban Power Plant . . . " *Montgomery County Magazine.* March 1992.

Robinson, Dick. "Captain Henry H. Talbot, 1841–1931." *Montgomery County Remembers.* Crawfordsville: Montgomery County Historical Society, 1976.

Ruby, Russell. "Trinity Church to Celebrate 100th Anniversary." *Montgomery County Magazine.* May 1994.

Salter, Mary A. "First Baptist Church to Celebrate 150th Year." *Montgomery County Magazine.* September 1988.

Sarver, Bina. "Smallpox Epidemic Hit Area in 1901." *Montgomery County Magazine.* March 1997.

Schup, Leonard. "Marshall Was Wabash Grad." *Montgomery County Magazine.* November 1988.

Seymour, Kathleen. "Stateley Elston Homestead . . . " *Montgomery County Remembers.* Crawfordsville: Montgomery County Historical Society, 1976.

Shortz, Wilma. "Horses Played Vital Role." *Montgomery County Legend and Lore.* Crawfordsville: Montgomery County Historical Society, 1988.

Spilman, Louis. "Thousands Saw City's First Plane Landing." *Montgomery County Remembers.* Crawfordsville: Montgomery County Historical Society, 1976.

Spragg, Joann. Curator at Lew Wallace Study. Interview on March 5, 2002.

———. "Wallace, Lincoln Crossed Paths Many Times." *Montgomery County Magazine.* May 1997.

———. "Wallace Organizes the Indiana Zouaves." *Montgomery County Magazine.* September 1999.

———. "Ben Hur Namesake Found From Music to Medicine." *Montgomery County Magazine.* November 1999.

"Sunshine Society Started in 1901." *Montgomery County Magazine.* December 1981.

Thomas, Trent. "Migration of Educators." *Montgomery County Legend and Lore.* Crawfordsville: Montgomery County Historical Society, 1988.

Thompson, Donald. "Ben Hur Affected Individuals." *Montgomery County Magazine.* February 1985.

———. "Lyons Music Company Celebrating 74th Year." *Montgomery County Magazine.* May 1989.

———. "Stephen Crane had Many Business Ventures." *Montgomery County Magazine.* April 1988.

———. "Sky Monster Alarmed Crawfordsville Residents." *Montgomery County Magazine.* May 1988.

———. W.C. Hurt in Spanish-American War." *Montgomery County Magazine.* December 1988.

———. "Woman Suffrage Group Organizes." *Montgomery County Magazine.* May

1987.

———. "City Proud of Title." *Montgomery County Magazine*. July 1982.

———. "Early Baseball League had Strong Local Support." *Montgomery County Magazine*. January 1988.

———. "Enoch Smith—Noted Author, Minister." *Montgomery County Magazine*. June 1983.

———. "Junction Was Busy Place in Railroad's Hey-Day!" *Montgomery County Magazine*. May 1990.

———. "Minetta Taylor Ranked High as a Writer." *Montgomery County Magazine*. April 1983.

———. "Mary H. Krout Was Noted Writer." *Montgomery County Magazine*. January 1886.

———. "Travel Often Difficult for Early County Residents." *Montgomery County Magazine*. June 1990.

———. "Wabash College Joins U.S. Military Program." *Montgomery County Magazine*. July 1988.

———. "William McKee Dunn was Active in Politics." *Montgomery County Magazine*. December 1989.

Thompson, Jean. "Historians unaware of city's first incorporation." *Montgomery County Magazine*. August 1990.

Trippet, Byron K. *Wabash On My Mind*. Crawfordsville: Wabash, 1982.

Wallace, Lew. "Wallace Shares Memories of Maurice Thompson." *Montgomery County Magazine*. August 1992.

Wernle, Robert F. "The Team That Tackled Old Jim Crow." *Montgomery County Magazine*. January 1998.

Whalen, Bob. "Two of CHS's Great teams are Remembered." *This Sunday*. 11 February 2002.

"What Crawfordsville Has." *Crawfordsville Journal*. 16 December 1910.

White, Alberta. "4-H Sprang from America's Concern for Youth." *Montgomery County Magazine*. August 1984.

White, Jean. "Girl Scouts to Celebrate 75th Anniversary." *Montgomery County Magazine*. March 1987.

Williams, Jean. "Crawfordsville Art League Celebrates 100th Anniversary." *Montgomery County Magazine*. April 1996.

Wyatt, Jack. "Camp Rotary . . . " *Montgomery County Magazine*. April 1990.

Zach, Karen. "Casket Plant Operated Here More than 100 years." *Montgomery County Magazine*. March 1990.

———. "Good Brothers Buses were a Success." *Montgomery County Magazine*. April 1999.

———. "Local Klub Popular." *Montgomery County Magazine*. May 1982.

———. *Montgomery Medicine Men and Women born 1850 or Before*. Crawfordsville: Montgomery County Historical Society, 2002.

———. "Taxicab Business Flourished in Crawfordsville." *Montgomery County Magazine*. January 1990.

Index